THE BEST WISCONSIN SPORTS ARGUMENTS

THE 100 MOST CONTROVERSIAL, DEBATABLE QUESTIONS FOR DIE-HARD FANS

ANDY KENDEIGH

SOURCEBOOKS, INC.®
NAPERVILLE, ILLINOIS

Published by Sourcebooks, Inc.
P.O. Box 4410, Naperville, Illinois 60567-4410
(630) 961-3900
Fax: (630) 961-2168
www.sourcebooks.com

Library of Congress Cataloging-in-Publication Data

Kendeigh, Andy.
   The best Wisconsin sports arguments : the 100 most controversial,
debatable questions for die-hard fans / by Andy Kendeigh.
      p. cm.
   1. Sports--Wisconsin--History--Miscellanea. 2. Sports records--Wis-
consin. I. Title.
   GV584.W6K46 2009
   796.09775--dc22
                           2009025670

Printed and bound in the United States of America.
VP 10 9 8 7 6 5 4 3 2 1

For the best team in town: my wife Wendy, and my girls: Sammy, Carly, and the baby.

CONTENTS

THE BUCKS

OUTSIDE THE LINES

HITS AND MISSES

ACKNOWLEDGMENTS

I would like to say thank you to the Hearst Corporation, especially WISN general manager Jan Wade and WISN news director Lori Waldon for allowing me to pursue this project and for their support.

Special thanks to my friends and colleagues for their insight and wisdom in helping me formulate these debates: Dan Needles, Stephanie Sutton, Hank Strunk, Jason Hunter, Carol Hunter, Dan Joerres, Lance Hill, Brian Lammi, John Lazarevic, Tim Van Vooren, Bob Brainerd, Drew Olson, Jason Wilde, Tom Oates, Jay Wilson, Steve True, Chris Roth, Pat Mayo, John Gillespie, Michelle Tuckner, Dan Smyczek, Rick Schlesinger, Tyler Barnes, Rob Reischel, Aaron Knight, Clark Vance, John Summers, Jim Tretow, Adam Woullard, Jeff Blumb, Sarah Quick, Joe Sweeney, and Eddie Erkmanis.

This book would not be possible without Pete Alfini and the folks at Sourcebooks. Thank you to my editors Kelly Bale and Shana Drehs: you are the best.

To my family, thank you for putting up with my long nights and cranky mornings. Thank you to my wife Wendy for her love and support. Thank you to my daughters Sammy and Carly for letting "daddy write." Thank you to Fran "Nana" Mott for watching my girls and allowing me the time to write. Thank you to my sounding board: my brothers John and Paul, my sisters Kit and Anne, and their families. Thank you to my parents Don and Lyn, who always encouraged my passion for sports.

And thank you to the sports fans in the great state of Wisconsin. Without you, this book would not exist.

INTRODUCTION

There are a handful of sports moments in life after which you can remember exactly where you were and what you were doing. It's as if time stood still for that event, a "remember-when" moment. For example, I know that when the Badgers won their first Rose Bowl on New Years Day 1994, I was at WKOW-TV, where I watched every play with my college roommate, Aaron Knight. Watching Darrell Bevell elude UCLA's defense for that memorable touchdown was something I will never forget. That moment defined the Barry Alvarez era and ranks as one of the best in state history—but there are others.

Maybe you can remember where you were when Brett Favre hooked up with Andre Rison in Super Bowl XXXI. You can still see Favre running, helmet in hand, his ear-to-ear grin setting the tone for the Packers' first Super Bowl title in almost three decades.

Or perhaps your moment was the Brewers winning the American League pennant back in 1982. You can picture Cecil Cooper begging the ball to find grass instead of leather.

Maybe your moment was Al McGuire's moment: the Marquette head coach crying on the bench in the closing moments of the 1977 NCAA Championship Game—his final game—as the Warriors won their only national championship. Or maybe it was MU's Final Four run in 2003. Or perhaps it was Wisconsin's Cinderella story in the 2000 NCAA Tournament, as the Badgers reached the Final Four.

Is pro hoops your thing? Maybe your moment is when the Bucks won their one and only championship in just their third season in the NBA.

That's what this book is all about—great moments and great debates in Wisconsin sports. It's about the best and the worst. You might not agree with everything you read, but there's little question you will have an opinion. That's what makes these arguments. I contend that Wisconsin is one of the most underrated sports states in the country. What's undeniable is the state's abundance of incredible, memorable sports moments to rejoice, bemoan, and argue over.

With that, here are the top 100 Wisconsin sports arguments.

LEADING OFF

WHAT'S THE GREATEST MOMENT IN WISCONSIN SPORTS HISTORY?

1 The state's greatest moments center on Wisconsin's favorite team, the Green Bay Packers. The two greatest wins in Packers history have to be the NFL Championship Game on New Year's Eve 1967, now known as the "Ice Bowl," and Super Bowl XXXI on January 26, 1997. The two victories exemplified two great periods for the Green Bay Packers—the Vince Lombardi era and the Brett Favre era.

The Packers went 29 years between winning Super Bowl II and Super Bowl XXXI. It was during the 1996 season when fans across the state could truly say, "The Pack is back!" After a 13–3 regular season and wins against the San Francisco 49ers and Carolina Panthers in the NFC playoffs, the Packers beat the New England Patriots at the Superdome in New Orleans in Super Bowl XXXI. Thousands of Packers fans turned Bourbon Street upside down after Brett Favre threw for two touchdowns, Reggie White recorded a record three sacks, and the game's Most

Valuable Player, Desmond Howard, returned a kickoff 99 yards for a key third-quarter touchdown to give the Packers their first championship in three decades by a score of 35–21. It was a watershed moment for a new Packers generation.

The previous generation's glory moment lacked the spectacle that surrounds a Super Bowl. In fact, the Ice Bowl was not a Super Bowl. Many fans forget that back in the late 1960s, the NFL championship was more coveted than winning what was then known as the AFL-NFL Championship Game—later, the Super Bowl. It was a foregone conclusion that the NFL champion would beat anyone from the upstart AFL. Yes, the Packers won the first two Super Bowls, but it was their victory which earned them a spot in Super Bowl II that is the greatest moment in Wisconsin sports history.

On the final day of 1967, Lambeau Field turned into a freezer as the Packers and Dallas Cowboys played in the coldest game in NFL history, with a game-time temperature of −13°F. With the wind chill, it felt like −46°F. It was so cold that the officials' whistles froze and did not work. Lambeau Field's $80,000, state-of-the-art heating system failed, though legend has it that Packers head coach Vince Lombardi turned off the system to give his team an advantage. Somehow, Bart Starr managed to throw two first-half touchdowns to Boyd Dowler, but it was the end of a 12-play, 68-yard drive that defined the game and an era. Starr put an end to this nail-biter when he called his own number, sneaking in from the 1-yard line with 13 seconds left to lead the Packers to a 21–17 victory.

The Ice Bowl symbolized the Lombardi Packers: tough, smart football players who worked together to win title after title—five to be exact (including the first two Super Bowls). It also exemplified the hardcore Packers fans, who were happy to brave the icy elements to cheer their team on to victory. Yes, thousands of Packers fans showed their dedication and spirit by traveling to the Big Easy for Super Bowl XXXI, but let's be honest: a trip to New Orleans in late January is an easy sell for any Packers fan braving another Wisconsin winter. Plus, the way the Green and Gold dominated the NFL in 1996, most fans figured it would be the first of a run of titles for the Mike Holmgren– and Brett Favre–led Packers. It was disappointing they did not win more. Sure, the win against the Patriots was outstanding—however, the Ice Bowl victory was the last Lombardi-coached Packers game in Green Bay. It's the most memorable for how the game was won and the elements in which it was played.

2 Hank Aaron? Number 44. Oscar Robertson? Number 1. Ron Dayne? Number 33. Robin Yount? Number 19. A player's number is an extension of the player himself. It's part of his personality. There's no greater sports number in the state of Wisconsin than the number 4. In fact, the three professional sports teams in the state all have retired the number 4. Of the three, which number 4, played his game the best?

BUCKS: SIDNEY MONCRIEF

Sidney Moncrief was the face of the franchise during an underappreciated era of Bucks basketball. Moncrief was the backbone of a team that won 523 games in the 1980s. His teams won 50 or more games for seven straight seasons, and he led the Bucks to the playoffs in each of his 10 seasons with the club. He was one of the game's dominant defenders. Moncrief won the NBA's first Defensive Player of the Year Award back in 1983, and was named to the NBA's All-Defensive First Team for four straight seasons. The man known as "Sir Sid" is the second-leading scorer in Bucks history, behind Kareem Abdul-Jabbar. Moncrief had his number 4 retired on January 6, 1990.

BREWERS: PAUL MOLITOR

"The Ignitor" played 12 seasons with the Milwaukee Brewers and led the Brew Crew to their one and only World Series appearance in 1982. Molitor is best known for his 39-game hitting streak in 1987, for a Brewers club nicknamed "Team Streak." Molitor was a five-time All-Star as a member of the Brewers, and he eventually finished his career with 3,319 hits, ranking him in the top 10 on baseball's all-time hits list. Molitor joined Robin Yount in 2004 as the only Brewers in the Baseball Hall of Fame and had his number 4 retired by the Brewers on July 11, 1999.

PACKERS: BRETT FAVRE

Favre wore number 10 at North Hancock High School but was given number 4 at Southern Mississippi, and he kept that number throughout his professional career. The number so identified Favre that during interviews, his teammates would just refer to him as "Four," as in, "When you have Four behind center, you are always in the game." When Favre was traded to the Jets, he already held almost every NFL career passing record, including 442 touchdown passes, 5,377 completions, 8,758 attempts, and 61,655 yards—all NFL records. He played in 255 straight regular-season games with the Packers, making

253 straight starts—275 straight starts when you add in his playoff appearances. To put it in perspective, if you were born the day Favre started his streak, you would be close to finishing high school by the end of it. Favre was named to nine Pro Bowls as a Packer, and led Green Bay to a victory in Super Bowl XXXI. His jersey is the best-selling Packers jersey of all time. A spot will be reserved for him at the Pro Football Hall of Fame in Canton, Ohio, when he eventually becomes eligible. For some, Favre's star faded a bit with the way his comeback and eventual trade were handled before the 2008 season. But there's no denying his impact on the Packers.

THE VERDICT

Two of the three number 4's are or will be in their sports' halls of fame: Paul Molitor and Brett Favre. Only Favre would be in the conversation as the best player of his respective sport. Molitor was fantastic but spent the bulk of his twilight years playing elsewhere as a designated hitter. Favre was in the upper echelon until he finally stepped away while playing his game's most important position. Favre was a game-changer and connected with fans like no other athlete in state history. When he was traded to the Jets, some fans continued to attend Packers games at Lambeau Field wearing Favre's Jets jersey while still cheering for the home team. The team had to postpone retiring Favre's number, but it will eventually make him the sixth Packer to be so honored. The number 4 is No. 1 in Wisconsin sports, and Favre is the leader of the Pack.

WHO BELONGS ON THE MOUNT RUSHMORE OF WISCONSIN SPORTS?

3 Four faces: George Washington, Thomas Jefferson, Theodore Roosevelt, and Abraham Lincoln. It's one of America's great monuments, representing four key presidents who helped shape the United States of America. What if sports in the state of Wisconsin had its own Mount Rushmore? Which four faces would adorn our monument?

The first two are easy: Vince Lombardi and Brett Favre. Two Packers. One coach and one player. One image representing the Packers dynasty of the 1960s, and the other carrying the green and gold torch into the new millennium. Half of the four faces are Packers, you ask? Absolutely, since no team in the state dominates the sports landscape like the NFL team that calls Titletown home.

It's tougher to come up with the two others to flank Lombardi and Favre. Kareem Abdul-Jabbar and Oscar Robertson led the Bucks to their one and only NBA title, but Kareem never really embraced the city of Milwaukee, and Oscar came to town late in his career. So, no Bucks on this Mount. Rushmore.

Baseball certainly needs to be represented on the mountaintop of Wisconsin sports. But who? How about Robin Yount and Paul Molitor, the two greatest Brewers? Both collected more than 3,000 hits and both are Hall of Fame ballplayers. It's a tough call picking one over the other. Thankfully, it's not necessary, since one of the greatest players who ever lived once called Milwaukee home. He's a man who many feel is baseball's true "home-run king." In the state of Wisconsin, there's no greater ambassador for baseball and the history of the sport than Hank Aaron.

Aaron spent his first 12 seasons and final two years playing for Milwaukee's major league team. In his career, "The Hammer" hit 755 home runs while Yount and Molitor combined for 485. Aaron collected 3,771 hits in his 23 seasons and finished with a career batting average of .305. Molitor was a point higher in his career average, but he had 450 fewer hits than Aaron. Yount's numbers trail Molitor with a .285 career average and 3,142 career hits. Aaron was also a better fielder, winning the Gold Glove Award three times while Yount and Molitor only have one between them. Three players are worthy, but only one can represent baseball on Wisconsin's Mount Rushmore, and that man is Henry Aaron.

Lombardi, Favre, Aaron and…? There is one spot left and two great college coaches to choose from: Barry Alvarez and Al McGuire. Much like Alvarez and the University of Wisconsin, McGuire was the face of his university—he *was*

Marquette. Even after his coaching career ended with a national title, McGuire and Marquette were linked forever. McGuire's Warriors won almost 79 percent of their games during his 13 years as head coach, as well as a national championship in 1977 and an NIT title in 1970. (They were the NCAA runners-up in 1974.) McGuire remained in the spotlight as a TV analyst long after he was done coaching. He was Dick Vitale before Dick Vitale. McGuire was the voice of college basketball.

Alvarez built the Wisconsin football program from scratch. He turned the Badgers into a perennial power and Camp Randall into a Saturday afternoon destination. Alvarez arrived in Madison on January 2, 1990, immediately after winning the national championship as Notre Dame's defensive coordinator. In just days, Alvarez sat on couch after couch, selling his vision to the best prep players in the state. He vowed to "build a wall" around Wisconsin to keep the best players home. In a little more than a month, Alvarez and his staff put together the foundation of a program in its fourth season that would play in the Rose Bowl for the first time in 31 years.

Alvarez led the Badgers to three Rose Bowl championships and is the only Big Ten coach to win back-to-back Rose Bowls. Twice, Alvarez was named National Coach of the Year. His teams appeared in 11 bowl games and won 8. He owns the best bowl-game winning percentage in college football history. Alvarez never did win a

11

national championship at Wisconsin, but he not only led the Badgers back to respectability, but to heights even the biggest Badger booster could not imagine. Alvarez literally changed the face of UW athletics. He was the one who changed the Badger logo from the plain, block, capital W to the dynamic, motion W which is now synonymous with Badger sports. Alvarez awoke a sleeping giant, which led to unprecedented national attention. After his coaching days ended, he took over for Pat Richter as Wisconsin's athletic director and even did some television commentary of his own, working bowl games for FOX.

If there were room for five faces on Wisconsin's Mount Rushmore, both McGuire and Alvarez could sit side by side, but since there can only be four, Alvarez gets the nod for his contributions both on and off the field and his impact on the largest university in the state. In the end, we would have two legendary coaches and two Hall of Fame players represented on the state's mountaintop of sports: Vince Lombardi, Brett Favre, Hank Aaron, and Barry Alvarez.

WHO BELONGS ON THE MOUNT RUSHMORE OF WISCONSIN SPORTS VOICES?

4 Sports fans in Wisconsin are a fortunate bunch. We have been blessed with some terrific and legendary voices of the game. This Mount Rushmore is reserved for the men who delivered the magic moments for your favorite teams over the years. Analysts like Larry McCarren and Max McGee of the Packers are left out, since this list is reserved for the men who called the play-by-play for the action.

You know the list is good when you see the group of guys who didn't quite make it onto the Mount Rushmore of Wisconsin sports voices—guys like Wayne Larivee, the versatile and excitable wordsmith currently behind the microphone for the Packers radio network. And who can think of the Badgers without thinking of Matt LePay? Ted Davis and Jim Paschke are gentlemen who can make Bucks losses entertaining. When Bucks fans think of their one and only championship, the man who brought that title to life was the longtime voice of the Bucks, Eddie Doucette.

You can't think of high school sports and television coverage of state tournament play without picturing Jay Wilson. Marquette fans have a great voice in Steve "the Homer" True. An impressive list, no doubt, but here are your four faces behind the legendary voices of Wisconsin sports.

Jim Irwin was the voice of the Packers for more than a quarter-century. He started in 1969 as the color analyst for six seasons before sliding over into the play-by-play chair. From 1975 to 1998, Irwin was the man who millions of Packers fans turned to on Sundays in the fall. Irwin was the state's Sportscaster of the Year 10 times and was inducted into the Wisconsin Broadcasters Association Hall of Fame in 1994.

Irwin is one of the few men to broadcast for all of the state's biggest teams, calling games throughout his career for the Packers, the Badgers, the Brewers, and the Bucks. But it is the Green Bay Packers that go hand in hand with Jim Irwin. He was there for the transition from Lombardi. He was there for the introduction and maturation of Brett Favre. Irwin was one of the first radio broadcasters for whom fans would actually turn down the television volume so they could turn up the radio and listen to his call of the action they were watching on TV. Irwin called a Brett Favre touchdown pass like no other, his voice raising with the stir and cheers in the stands. A reporter once asked Irwin what his most memorable game was, and without hesitation, he replied, "The NFC Championship Game in

January '97 against the Carolina Panthers here at Lambeau Field." Irwin said what made it so enjoyable was that the fourth quarter was as much a coronation as a competition. The game was in hand, and everyone in the stadium knew the Packers would be back on football's biggest stage, competing for the trophy bearing Lombardi's name. Irwin's call of running back Edgar Bennett plowing through the line for a late touchdown—running through a hole "big enough to drive a truck" to the Super Bowl—was one fans will always remember. The Super Bowl victory in New Orleans two weeks later was the icing on the cake for Irwin and the Packers.

Before Jim Irwin, there was Ray Scott, who was known as "the voice of the Green Bay Packers." Simply stated, if you are a Baby Boomer, your Packers voice was Ray Scott. If you are a member of Generation X, Jim Irwin was your guy. Ray Scott first broadcast Packers games on CBS television in 1956 and called Packers games until 1967, making him the voice of the Lombardi era. Back in those days, the network assigned an announcer to each team, and Scott was the Packers guy. His simplistic style resonated with Packers fans. Ray Scott simply called the action. "Starr to Dowler, touchdown," was the standard description of a Bart Starr touchdown pass to Boyd Dowler no matter how spectacular. It may sound boring by today's standards. However, Scott exemplified a simpler time, and his broadcasts gave listeners the basics. Unlike some of

15

today's broadcasters, Scott was never self-centered—his calls were strictly football. Like the others on this list, Scott was generous with his time and gave back to the community, serving as an emcee for countless banquets and local awards dinners. Scott called the Ice Bowl and four Super Bowls. He's the voice longtime Green Bay fans associate with the Packers dynasty of the 1960s. Scott also called two seasons of Brewers baseball on TV in the mid-1970s.

Earl Gillespie was known as "the voice of the Milwaukee Braves," but really, he did it all. He called Badger football games and Marquette basketball and football games. Gillespie even did play-by-play for the Green Bay Packers, which didn't last long, since the Packers were sponsored by Hamm's and the Braves were sponsored by Miller. Gillespie stuck with the Braves. He was one of the original broadcasters to use the phrase "holy cow" when describing the action. Gillespie was known for his charity work and his close affiliation with Children's Hospital in Milwaukee. He would always have his fishing net ready to catch any foul balls close to the broadcast booth—then he'd get players to sign the baseballs and hand-deliver the keepsakes to the sick kids. Gillespie's biggest thrill was calling the 1957 World Series, delivering the good news that the Milwaukee Braves were the best team in baseball.

Lastly, the guy who nicknamed himself "Mr. Baseball" is so good that he made the Brewers of the 1990s worth listening to. Bob Uecker was a star on a team with no stars. For more than 50 years, Uecker has been calling baseball games—the last 40 with the Milwaukee Brewers. Usually, a club puts its most marketable player on the cover of its media guide. The Brewers put Uecker on the cover in 2005. Not bad for a guy who hit .200 in his playing career! His style of self-depreciating humor is legendary, and yet, he never loses sight of why he's there—to give listeners the play-by-play of a baseball game. Uecker made himself a national name by appearing on the *Tonight Show* close to 100 times. He appeared in famous Miller Lite commercials, and even starred in his own sitcom, *Mr. Belvedere.* Uecker's best role on the silver screen came as Harry Doyle, the hard-drinking broadcaster in the *Major League* movies.

Like Gillespie, Uecker has given to countless charities, and every year, he holds a fishing tournament for the Make-A-Wish Foundation. He's one of the good guys in broadcasting—and one of the best. Uecker earned the 2003 Ford Frick Award and is recognized in the Baseball Hall of Fame, truly gaining a seat in the front row.

5 You can state your case for Dick Bennett's hiring at UW or Tom Crean's at Marquette. Let me hear Brewers fans clamor for Harvey Kuenn, who took over at midseason to lead the Brewers to their one and only American League pennant back in 1982. And let's not forget Bo Ryan being chosen to replace Brad Soderberg, who had taken over for Dick Bennett as the head coach of the Badgers basketball team. Mike Holmgren replacing Lindy Infante in Green Bay was a shrewd move, as well, but this argument comes down to two moves that changed the course of the history of sports in the state of Wisconsin—one in the college ranks and one in the pros.

DONNA SHALALA HIRES PAT RICHTER AT THE UNIVERSITY OF WISCONSIN

UW chancellor Donna Shalala knew that in order to lead a first-class university, she needed a first-class athletic department. So on December 15, 1989, Shalala plucked former Badger Pat Richter away from Oscar Meyer and brought him back to Monroe Street to lead the Badger athletic program into the 21st century. The fact that Richter was a successful businessman was equally as important as his athletic prowess. Richter was an All-American tight end back in the 1960s, but it was his business background that sealed the deal. This was the turning point for the UW athletic department that laid the foundation for a national powerhouse.

When he stepped into his new role as athletic director, Richter hit the ground running. It took him less than three weeks to hire Barry Alvarez, and it took Alvarez just four years to bring a Rose Bowl title to Madison. Football took the lead in changing the university's national sports reputation. For years, one of the few sports in which UW could count on being a perennial power was hockey. After Richter, and then Alvarez, Wisconsin finally became known as a football school that contended for a bowl game year in and year out.

Football success led to basketball success, and Wisconsin soon became an athletic power in the Big Ten. In addition, Richter took an athletic-department deficit of $2 million and turned it into a $6 million reserve. You can credit Donna Shalala for hiring him.

BOB HARLAN HIRES RON WOLF IN GREEN BAY

Back in 1991, the Packers were going nowhere fast. In the middle of a 4–12 season, Bob Harlan knew he needed to make a change. So on November 27, 1991, Harlan hired

Ron Wolf away from the New York Jets to become the Packers' general manager.

Wolf spent the final month of the 1991 season scouting players and realized Lindy Infante would not continue to coach the Packers. He sacked Infante and hired Mike Holmgren. Wolf then made one of the greatest trades in NFL history. He sent a future No. 1 draft pick to the Atlanta Falcons for a rookie quarterback—some kid named Brett Favre.

In 1993, Wolf completed the GM equivalent of a Hail Mary, signing the best defensive player in the game, free agent Reggie White. No one thought that White would come to Green Bay, but Wolf managed to pull it off. Reggie gave credit to God for directing him to Green Bay, but Wolf deserves his share of thanks, as well. White was wined and dined by many teams during free agency, but the well-researched Wolf took him out to dinner at Red Lobster so the big defensive end could eat his favorite food, catfish. The catfish and the no-nonsense approach to negotiations led White to sign a four-year, $17-million deal with the Packers.

With Reggie White and Brett Favre together, the Packers would finally put the "title" back into Titletown, winning Super Bowl XXXI. Ron Wolf never had a losing season in Green Bay, and it was that long-term success that led to the renovation of Lambeau Field, which keeps the Packers competitive as the smallest-market team in the NFL. You can thank Bob Harlan for the Ron Wolf hire that changed the face and the fate of the Green Bay Packers.

THE VERDICT

Which was the better hire? That's like picking a favorite child. Both were instrumental in turning around programs—one for the biggest university in the state, and the other for the most popular professional team in Wisconsin. The big difference between the two is that the Packers are obviously centered around the product on the field. The University of Wisconsin is based on academics, with athletics as an added bonus. No matter who Donna Shalala originally hired as Wisconsin's athletic director, UW would have continued on, whether there was athletic success in Madison or not. Pat Richter demonstrated how an athletic department can support and strengthen an already respected university.

The Packers, however, were a mess at that time of Wolf's hire. They were in danger of falling into an atmosphere of fan indifference and malaise. In the NFL's smallest market, no one truly knows what would have happened if Bob Harlan had hired someone other than Ron Wolf. If the Packers had continued to fail on the field, there's no telling how long the city of Green Bay would have continued supporting its team. Thankfully, we don't have to answer that question. Instead, Wolf was hired, which led to a return to Super Bowl glory, and then later, an upgrade to one of the finest facilities in the NFL, Lambeau Field. Ron Wolf was the most important hire in Wisconsin sports history.

WHICH WAS THE BETTER FRANCHISE-SAVING RENOVATION?

6 Both the Packers and the Brewers needed help near the end of the 20th century. Both teams needed new or renovated stadiums to stay competitive. Eventually, they both managed to get stadium deals done with help from the taxpayers. Lambeau Field's renovation cost $295 million, while Miller Park's price tag was just under $400 million. Which stadium plan was the better idea? Which franchise needed its stadium deal more?

In the early 1990s, George Petak was a Wisconsin state senator from Racine. His life changed after midnight on October 6, 1995, during an all-night session of the state legislature in Madison, when he dramatically switched his vote in favor of a 0.1 percent tax for those living in the five-county area around Milwaukee, projected to end by 2014, to help finance Miller Park. Petak's change of heart pushed the plan through the State Senate and got the ball rolling to build the Brewers' new home. However, his constituents were not happy. A year later, Petak became the first Wisconsin legislator to be recalled. Nevertheless, it's quite possible that without Petak's vote, the Brewers would be calling another city home. It was simply impossible for a small-market team like Milwaukee to survive without a new stadium. Instead, Petak's swing vote made it possible for Miller Park to open in 2001.

Public financing of sports stadiums makes most people uneasy. Some question a tax to help pay for a sports facility when the money could better serve elsewhere. No matter what your stance is on the tax issue, there's no question that the Brewers were desperate for a new home. County Stadium was a glorified minor-league ballpark, having stood for four decades but lacking the modern amenities. Major League Baseball commissioner Bud Selig, who owned the Brewers at the time, has said that Miller Park kept the Brewers in Milwaukee.

Like County Stadium but with more history, Lambeau Field near the end of the 20th century was in desperate need of a face life. Packers president Bob Harlan knew it had to be done. Lambeau Field was historic but old. It needed a face lift in the worst way. Without a new and improved facility, the Packers would not be able to generate the money to compete in the NFL. However, in the wake of the Miller Park debate, selling the public on another stadium tax was no easy feat, even in Green Bay. To make matters worse, the team stumbled out of the gate in the 2000 season under new head coach Mike Sherman, losing its first two games—the only two before the Lambeau Field referendum went to a vote.

Harlan worked tirelessly to sell the public on the idea, and his hard work paid off. The referendum passed, 53 percent to 47 percent in favor of a 0.5 percent sales tax in Brown County. Like Miller Park, the tax to help finance Lambeau Field is scheduled to end by 2014. Two stadiums were built, each to secure the future of a franchise. Both teams needed a new facility, but which needed it more?

The renovated Lambeau Field was a better idea as a structure and is the model stadium for new facilities in any sport. It's a modern stadium with all the bells and whistles—luxury boxes, an enormous atrium, a gift shop, a hall of fame, and multiple restaurants on site—but it was built without sacrificing any history. In fact, there's more history on display at the new Lambeau than the old one. Walking into the Lambeau Field Atrium is like taking a trip down memory lane on your way into seeing the modern-day Packers. Former head coach Mike Sherman added a nice touch when he insisted on taking concrete from the old Packers tunnel to the new tunnel (it was moved from the north end zone to the current location in the southeast corner). Now, when the Packers take the field every Sunday, they walk over the same concrete that Starr, Nitschke, Favre, and White walked on.

The night that the Lambeau Field renovation was passed, back in September 2000, a victory party was held at the Stadium View Bar, just down the street from Lambeau,

There, Bob Harlan said, "Everyone in the county should be congratulated for what you've saved tonight." Harlan could have congratulated the taxpayers for what they created on that night. The voters created an opportunity to build the best stadium surrounding the most historic field in the NFL. The Packers fans did not drop the ball.

Yet, the Brewers needed Miller Park even more than the Packers needed a renovated Lambeau Field for this reason: No matter the stadium vote, the NFL would have found some way to keep the Packers in Green Bay. The Packers helped build the NFL into what it is today. Lombardi's Packers of the 1960's rank as the greatest dynasty in pro football history. The league would have looked extremely greedy if it had let the Packers move to a bigger market like Los Angeles just to chase an extra buck. The team may not have been competitive, but it would have stayed put.

The same can't be said about the Brewers in Milwaukee. Major League Baseball had expanded in 1993, with the Colorado Rockies and Florida Marlins, and the league was getting ready to expand again in 1998, with the Arizona Diamondbacks and Tampa Bay Devil Rays (now the Tampa Bay Rays). If the Brewers had failed in their attempts to build a new home, there were plenty of cities that would have welcomed a new team with open arms. Miller Park saved the Brewers.

Which was more of a franchise-saving idea? As political as it was, the Brewers having their new stadium pushed through saved baseball in Milwaukee. County Stadium was iffy as a major-league ballpark in the 1960s—never mind by the mid-1990s. There was a need for a new stadium with new revenue streams to help the Brewers become competitive. As much as some did not like the way it was handled, it was necessary for baseball to thrive in Milwaukee. As the famous line from the movie *Field of Dreams* says, "If you build it, they will come." Perhaps George Petak heard the same mantra as he made his decision. There's no question he heard plenty of vocal opinions from both sides of the debate, but ultimately Petak had a change of heart and changed his vote in favor of a new stadium. Since Miller Park was built, the Brewers have set new attendance records as they've turned the franchise around. The building of Miller Park was a better franchise-saving renovation.

WHAT'S THE WORST IDEA IN WISCONSIN SPORTS HISTORY?

7 Can you imagine a school in the Big Ten Conference that doesn't play baseball? Or cheerleaders at baseball games? How about the Packers ending a long tradition of playing games in Milwaukee? UW's Circus Day? Favre's first retirement? What's the one common thread through these notions? They were all bad ideas surrounding sports played in Wisconsin.

In the late 1980s, the University of Wisconsin was known for bad football, and the Don Morton era at Wisconsin was defined by one bad promotion: Circus Day at Camp Randall. The halftime entertainment on that sunny Saturday in the late 1980s was a traveling circus, complete with an elephant. Evidently, the elephant was not a fan of the veer offense, as it decided to leave something behind near the Badgers' bench. The start of the second half was delayed so UW workers could power spray the elephant dung off the artificial turf.

In a different kind of sticky situation, UW had a major quandary in the early 1990s. It needed to conform to Title

IX, which gives male and female athletes equal access to intercollegiate sports. To do so, UW had to make some sacrifices. Dropping baseball was one of them. So in the spring of 1991, the Badgers played their last game on the diamond. It was a strange circumstance since the UW athletic director at the time was former Badgers baseball player (as well as football and basketball player) Pat Richter.

Let's not pile on UW. There are plenty of bad ideas to go around. Mark Attanasio brought competitive baseball back to Milwaukee, but he also signed off on cheerleaders, called "Diamond Dancers," at select Brewer games. Baseball needs pom-pon girls like the Racing Sausages need Randall Simon.

The Packers are not immune to bad ideas. Green Bay played a few home games every season in Milwaukee for 62 straight years (1933–1994) and often drew big crowds there, first at State Fair Park, and later at County Stadium, which allowed for bigger gate receipts. This eliminated the idea of placing another NFL team in a city only 100 miles south of Green Bay. However, by the mid-1990s, the rising costs of playing a "home" game away from home became too great. Lambeau Field had expanded over the years to the point where its capacity was greater than County Stadium. In 1995, the Packers decided all games would be played at Lambeau Field, ending a terrific tradition and disappointing thousands of fans of the Green and Gold in Milwaukee.

Speaking of green and gold, the Packers were once the Blue and Gold! When Curly Lambeau started the team, he brought his Notre Dame colors to Wisconsin. However, former head coach Gene Ronzani put the *green* in the Green Bay Packers and changed the uniforms from blue to green. The color scheme changed back and forth until Vince Lombardi got to town in 1961, and then it was green and gold forever—or at least until the 1990s, when General Manager Ron Wolf floated the idea of bringing the blue back to the Packers uniforms. Thankfully, it never got past the discussion phase, keeping Green Bay as the only NFL team with green and gold as its primary colors.

Sometimes, a Wisconsin team is the victim of a bad idea. In 2004, the University of Illinois basketball team insisted on wearing its home orange jerseys—instead of standard white—when playing the Badgers in Champaign. The problem was, Wisconsin's visiting cardinal red jerseys looked a lot like the orange. On television, it was tough to tell Devin Harris from Deron Williams. Depending on how large or small the TV was, a lot of people couldn't tell the difference at all. It was a terrible idea by Illinois, although it worked in the team's favor. The Badgers evidently had trouble figuring out who was who, since they turned the ball over 17 times in a 65–57 loss to the Illini.

These all pale in comparison to the worst idea in state sports history: The Marquette Gold. The school had been down this name-changing road 10 years before, in 1994, when the Warriors were turned into the Golden Eagles. The new nickname had trouble catching on, since most alumni wanted to keep the name *Warriors*. The debate took another twist in May 2004, when prominent alumnus Wayne Sanders offered $1 million if Marquette went back to being called the Warriors. School officials declined, but a name-change was on the horizon. Market research showed a tepid interest in the Golden Eagles nickname, and Marquette officials decided they needed an updated moniker—just not the Warriors. MU's board of trustees decided that *Gold* would be the new name, punctuated by university president Robert Wild telling a crowd of students gathered on campus, "We are Marquette... Gold!" The name lasted a week. The public outcry was so loud that the trustees went back to square one, reopened talks surrounding the mascot, and decided to hold a school-wide vote. The catch? The name *Warriors* was not an option. *Golden Eagles* won out and became the school's old-new nickname in the same month.

Gold might have lost, but it won the gold medal for bad ideas in Wisconsin sports.

WHERE'S THE BEST PLACE TO WATCH A LIVE SPORTING EVENT IN WISCONSIN?

8 The state of Wisconsin has its share of first-class sporting venues. From Lambeau Field to Camp Randall to Miller Park back to the old MECCA, there's no shortage of classic stadiums and arenas in the Badger state. However, which location is the best for fans to take in their sport?

Miller Park is one of the better baseball stadiums in the major leagues. For one, you know there will always be baseball played when it is scheduled, thanks to a retractable roof. In 2005, *Sports Illustrated* recognized Miller Park as the best fan value in the big leagues. The magazine has since turned the voting over to the fans and in 2008, Miller Park was still voted second-best fan value to Cleveland's Jacob's Field. The survey asked fans to consider categories like affordability, food quality, and promotions. (Notice there's no talk of County Stadium in this debate. The old home of the Braves, then the Brewers, had charm, which is a nice way of saying it was a glorified minor-league ballpark and had no business serving as home to a major-league baseball team.)

Basketball fans can take their pick of which arena is best. The Kohl Center gives Wisconsin a home-court advantage like no other. Every game is a sellout, and the student section, "the Grateful Red," is located courtside in the south end zone, just beyond the baseline, where fans give opponents an earful each time they move down the court. A sold-out Bradley Center for a Marquette game could be the loudest venue in the state. The MECCA is one of college basketball's classics, first serving as home to Marquette, and now to UW–Milwaukee. The Resch Center in Green Bay gives the UWGB a first-class modern facility.

Tucked in the west side of UW's campus, Camp Randall Stadium gives big-time college football a neighborhood feel. Autumn Saturdays in Madison are tough to beat, with thousands of Badgers fans clad in red and white tailgating wherever they can find the space. In 2005, the $109 million renovation made improvements without sacrificing the structure. Add in all the traditions on football Saturdays, from Jump Around, to the slow-motion wave, to the Fifth Quarter, and taking in a Badgers game at Camp Randall is a must for any college football fan.

Lambeau Field is without question one of the greatest stadiums in professional sports. Any reporter who covers the NFL for a living would agree the Packers home ranks as one of, if not the best, facility in the NFL. Bob Harlan deserves the credit here. The former Packers president helped sway the vote in favor of renovating Lambeau Field just after the turn of the century, ensuring a permanent home for professional football in the NFL's smallest market. The renovation of Lambeau Field cost almost $300 million, but it was worth every penny. It blends the past with the present, preserving history with statues of Vince Lombardi and Curly Lambeau flanking the Atrium on its north side and housing the Packers Hall of Fame inside. The stadium itself is one of the best since every seat in the house is a good seat. However, it's not *the* best.

One hour north of Milwaukee and just over an hour south of Green Bay sits Whistling Straits, in the tiny, unincorporated community of Haven. The Straits was the brainchild of Herb Kohler and was designed by Pete Dye. This public facility is one of the best and most beautiful golf courses in the country. It sits on the shores of Lake Michigan, so 8 of the 18 holes at Whistling Straits hug the shoreline of the Great Lake. The rolling links–style course harkens back to an earlier era in golf. There's even a flock of Scottish blackface sheep roaming the course. Opened in 1998, Whistling Straits quickly jumped into the rotation of hosting major championships on the PGA Tour. In 2004, Vijay Singh won the PGA Championship there as the Straits set attendance records.

The beauty of watching golf at Whistling Straits is twofold: One, the picturesque background is breathtaking. Two, the hills give the spectators literally thousands of opportunities to get an elevated view. Very few venues give fans the chance to get so close to the action with general-admission tickets. The PGA Tour agrees, since it has awarded the PGA Championship to Whistling Straits in 2010 and 2015, and the course will host the prestigious Ryder Cup in 2020. Just one word of caution—with all the hills, there were dozens of sprained ankles for the uninitiated at the 2004 PGA Championship. However, with views that good for watching the greatest golfers in the world, Whistling Straits takes the title of best sports venue in the state of Wisconsin.

WHERE'S THE BEST TAILGATING IN WISCONSIN?

9 One thing all sports fans in Wisconsin can agree on is that everyone loves tailgating. The practice of eating, drinking, and socializing with friends before a big game is a crucial ingredient for many to maximize their game-day experience. The term *tailgating* in Wisconsin has a relatively loose definition. It's the gathering of like-minded people before or after a sporting event, usually with drinks and food at the ready. It doesn't require an actual tailgate anymore.

Packers fans have huge parking lots surrounding Lambeau Field to use. Plus, neighborhood homes serve as hosts to many pregame parties. Rain or shine, warm but mostly cold, the pregame tailgate off Lombardi Avenue is a staple for Packers fans. If you are fortunate enough to have a parking pass in the Lambeau Field lot, there's no greater tailgating backdrop in sports. Even without a pass, you can park in the neighborhood lots surrounding the Packers' home—some spots are on front lawns, with the "tailgate" parties in backyards—so the pregame parties before a Packers game literally stretch for blocks.

With space at a premium surrounding Camp Randall Stadium in Madison, the neighborhood homes on Breeze Terrace serve as party headquarters before and after Badgers football games. Again, a permit is mandatory for any parking lot within a short walk of the stadium, so some fans choose to "tailgate" at one of the handful of establishments within a block of Camp Randall.

Miller Park is another terrific site to grill, drink, and play. Tailgating was perhaps the single greatest advantage to building Miller Park on the site of the now-demolished County Stadium rather than in downtown Milwaukee. The huge parking lots surrounding the stadium turn Miller Park into the state's biggest sports bar 81 times a year—something that would be impossible at a downtown stadium site. Plus, parking near the stadium is open to everyone—the earlier you arrive, the better the spot you will get. There are five enormous lots within a short walk to the stadium, and Miller Park makes a terrific backdrop for any pregame get-together. The sport of baseball lends itself to tailgating, giving it a more relaxed, laid-back, party atmosphere—before a football game, the pregame partying is a bit more intense due to the nature of the contest that fans are about to watch.

The best tailgating would be a mix of all three sites. In a perfect world, you get to Miller Park early, set up the grill, lay out the spread, and start playing games like Baggo or ball golf with the music pumping in the shadows of the ballpark.

After the game ended, we'd head to the parking lots at Lambeau Field for the postgame barbecue: more food, more drink, and conversation about a big Packers victory.

To cap the perfect tailgating day, we'd walk across Monroe Street to Stadium Bar, which most Badgers fans know as the former Jingles Bar. The parking lot surrounding the building would turn into an outdoor barroom, with only a chain-link fence separating the tailgaters from the street. The music would get louder as fans broke down the key plays of a Badgers victory. It would be the first of multiple stops—from Jingles to the Big 10 Pub, down to the Regent Street Retreat, then on to Bucks, barhopping in Madison is a game-day tradition. Finally, we'd make our way down to State Street to help the night turn to day, since Madison is the place to cap a fruitful fantasy day of tailgating.

THE PACKERS

IS GREEN BAY STILL "TITLETOWN"?

10 June and July are the dog days in sports television. NFL training camps don't start until late July, pro basketball has just finished up, and, aside from regular-season baseball and the majors in golf and tennis on the weekends, there's a void in the sports landscape. To fill that void, in the summer of 2008, ESPN conducted a month-long series, complete with an online fan vote, to determine which city deserved the moniker, "Titletown, USA." The winner? Valdosta, Georgia. Green Bay finished third.

For years, Green Bay has been known as Titletown, and for good reason, since the Packers own 12 NFL championships. However, with just one since the 1967 season, does Green Bay still deserve to be called Titletown?

In 2003, *ESPN the Magazine* fan satisfaction survey ranked the Green Bay Packers the best franchise in the country among the 121 teams in the four major sports (football, baseball, basketball, and hockey). Also in 2003, *Street & Smith's SportsBusiness Journal* named the Packers the world's best-run sports franchise. In 2004, *Sports Illustrated* conducted a poll among NFL players, who named the Green Bay Packers the classiest organization in the league.

Green Bay, Wisconsin (population 102,313), is the smallest market in big-time sports. It's the one city in America where's there's a unified, no-doubt-about-it, top dog in town. It's the Packers, 24/7, 365 days a year. When the Packers win, Green Bay mornings are not so chilly. When the Packers lose, those mornings are a cold right hook to the face.

Packers fans love the weather. Summertime in Green Bay is marvelous, although very short. In Green Bay, it's winter almost all of the time and the bad weather is legendary—everyone knows the Ice Bowl was played on the "frozen tundra." Packers fans pride themselves on cheering in the elements. You can picture Vince Lombardi standing on the sidelines with his long coat and fur hat—you could see his breath even during the day. Picture Brett Favre blowing into his hands before taking a snap, and then after the play, immediately putting them back into the pouch sewn below the number 4 on the front of his jersey. The Packers play in historic Lambeau Field, which was renovated in 2003 to bring the stadium into the 21st century without losing any history.

It's tough to argue with 12 championships (1929–1931, 1936 1939, 1944, 1961, 1962, 1965–1967, and 1996). That's three more titles than any other team in the NFL (the Chicago Bears have nine). The NFL even named the

41

Super Bowl trophy after Vince Lombardi. That's tradition. However, even with Brett Favre at quarterback, the Packers have only one championship since Lombardi's final game with Green Bay, Super Bowl II, on January 14, 1968.

The Packers have the unique distinction of not having an owner. The fans own the team. Currently, 112,088 people (representing 4,750,936 shares) own the Green Bay Packers. The last stock offering came in 1997–1998, when the Packers raised $24 million by adding 105,989 shareholders at $200 a share.

Lambeau Field has been sold out since 1960. More than 75,000 Packers fans remain on the waiting list. That means there are more fans on the waiting list to sit in Lambeau Field than there are actually sitting in Lambeau Field on game day (capacity 72,928).

Can you take away a nickname? The answer is no. Robin Yount is still "the Kid," even though he's closer to getting an AARP card than being on a baseball card. Glenn Robinson is still "the Big Dog," even if later in his career, his game lacked bite. Even though it's been a while since the Packers last raised the Lombardi Trophy, Green Bay is still Titletown, USA, no matter how many folks in Valdosta, Georgia, vote online.

WHICH WAS THE BEST PACKERS TEAM?

11 The Packers own 12 NFL championships, but which team is the best of the best? The 1996 team gets consideration for winning 16 of 19 games, including Super Bowl XXXI. That squad finished as the NFL's top-ranked offense, as well as defense. The team's three losses all came on the road to teams with winning records (Dallas, Minnesota, and Kansas City). But even with the outstanding record, it's remarkable that only Reggie White and Brett Favre are considered locks for the Hall of Fame. The Lombardi Packers were loaded with Hall of Famers like Bart Starr, Jim Taylor, Paul Hornung, Forrest Gregg, Ray Nitschke, Willie Davis, Jim Ringo, and Willie Wood.

The only undefeated Packers team played in 1929, under the direction of Curly Lambeau. The 1929 squad went 12–0–1, but a couple of its wins came against teams like the Dayton Triangles and the Providence Steam Roller—not exactly football as we know it. Plus, back then, the NFL did not have a postseason—the championship was simply awarded to the team with the best regular-season record.

Vince Lombardi's championship team of 1966 deserves consideration. That club went 12–2 in the regular season and would go on to beat the Chiefs in Super Bowl I. Including the playoffs, the 1966 team outscored its opponents 404–200.

However, the best of the best is the 1962 Packers team. That year, Vince Lombardi led the Packers to a 13–1 record, and they beat the Giants 16–7 for the second of his five titles. That club won 14 of 15 games and outscored its opponents 431–155. Those Packers had the highest-scoring offense and stingiest defense in the NFL. If it wasn't for a Thanksgiving Day loss at Detroit, the Packers would have gone undefeated. Jim Taylor, Bart Starr, Willie Wood, and Paul Hornung were all in their prime. Lombardi was, too. They won their first three games by a combined score of 100–7. The 1962 Packers team was the best of Lombardi's five title teams and the best club in franchise history.

FOR ONE GAME, WHO'S YOUR QUARTERBACK, FAVRE OR STARR?

12 If there's one team that unifies the state of Wisconsin, it's the Green Bay Packers. Churches schedule masses around Packers games. College basketball schedules have been reworked so they avoid competing with Packers games. The Packers are always the biggest sports story, week in and week out, even during the off-season. Any television news director in Wisconsin will tell you that there are two things that dominate news coverage in the state: the weather and the Green Bay Packers.

Two players define the franchise: Bart Starr and Brett Favre—both quarterbacks, both Hall of Famers, and both strangely successful playing in Wisconsin's elements. Each played 16 seasons in Titletown. Between them, they won six NFL championships and four NFL MVP Awards. So if you had one game to win, and needed one quarterback to win it for you, who would you choose, number 15 or number 4?

STARR

Bart Starr was the quintessential Vince Lombardi player. He was a quiet leader, cerebral yet able to lift his teammates to another level. Starr was an afterthought in the 1956 draft, selected in the 17th round out of Alabama. In fact, Starr would not even have been drafted today, since the modern draft lasts a mere seven rounds. But Starr managed to work his way into the starting lineup, and when Vince Lombardi came to Green Bay in 1959, Starr was able to guide a dynasty to five NFL championships, including victories in the first two Super Bowls.

Starr didn't have a rocket arm, but he was the perfect quarterback for Lombardi's system. He was smart, he called his own plays, and he was more than capable physically to execute all of the throws required. Like Favre, Starr was tough and was clutch, exemplified by his most notable win in the famous Ice Bowl in 1967, when the Packers beat the Cowboys at Lambeau Field, battling a wind chill of −46°F. Starr made the decision to sneak the ball in from the 1-yard line with no time outs and just 13 seconds remaining in the game. The original play was "35-wedge," a running play for Chuck Mercein. Instead of handing the ball off, Starr followed the lead block behind guard Jerry Kramer, and the Packers were victorious in the coldest game in NFL history.

Bart Starr lost just one playoff game in his career—his first one, the 1960 NFL Championship Game against the

Philadelphia Eagles. Starr finished his career 9–1 in the postseason and was the MVP of the first two Super Bowls.

FAVRE

Of all the records Brett Favre holds, he once said the record which meant the most was his iron-man streak. Favre started 253 straight regular-season games for the Packers—275 if you count playoff games. To put that in perspective, 64 different quarterbacks started at least one game in the 2007 regular season. However, for the Green Bay Packers, from week 4 in 1992 through the NFC Championship Game in January 2008, there was only one starter at quarterback: Brett Favre. When he first retired, Favre owned almost every NFL passing record in the book: most touchdowns, most passing yards, most passing attempts, most completions, and most wins. And of course, he also holds the record for most consecutive games started at football's most dangerous position, quarterback. He battled through a broken thumb on his throwing hand, a sprained knee ligament, a sprained foot, multiple concussions, and tendinitis. In his 16 seasons in Green Bay, Favre was listed on the injury report for 50 weeks, which works out to more than three full seasons. For those 16 years, he was there playing his heart out every week.

Fans loved Favre because they could relate to him. He was human. He had a drinking problem; he went to rehab to beat an addiction to painkillers; his house was hit by a tornado; and his boyhood home in Mississippi was hit by Hurricane Katrina. Favre had everyday problems that played out in front of everyone. His most emotional game came on a Monday night in Oakland in December 2003. The night before, Favre's father, Irv, had died of a heart attack, and no one would have blamed him if he had wanted to grieve on his own, away from football. Instead, Favre paid tribute to his father by playing the best game of his career. He threw for four touchdowns and 399 yards as the Packers crushed the Raiders. Favre said he thought his dad would have wanted him to play.

Favre also threw an NFL-record 288 interceptions, and his reputation for being a "gunslinger" at times would catch up with him. Some of his picks were season-ending. The overtime pass in Philadelphia, on January 11, 2004, in the NFC Divisional Game, which led to a painful end to the "Fourth and 26" game was one. And who could forget the very last pass of Brett Favre's Packers career? It was the interception in overtime against the New York Giants which cost Green Bay the NFC championship on January 20, 2008.

THE VERDICT

So which quarterback would you want behind center if you had one game to win? My answer is Bart Starr. He was simply more consistent in big games. He won 9 of the 10 postseason games he played in. Favre was an above-average quarterback in the playoffs, finishing his Packers career with a 12–10 postseason record, but with him, you never knew what you were going to get. For every play that made you say, "How did he do that?" there was also one that made you groan, "How could he do that?" Favre is, without question, the most entertaining quarterback I have ever seen but if I needed one quarterback to win one game, I'd choose Bart Starr.

WHICH WAS THE BIGGER HEART-BREAKER, 4TH AND 26 OR THE 2008 NFC CHAMPIONSHIP GAME?

13 The Packers' loss to the Denver Broncos in Super Bowl XXXII is, hands down, the most disappointing loss in state history. Tough to argue about that, since Green Bay entered that game as defending Super Bowl champions and a double-digit favorite, only to watch Mike Shanahan concoct a brilliant game plan that earned John Elway his first of two Super Bowl titles. The magnitude of the game and the missed opportunity to become back-to-back champs still sticks in the craw of Packers fans from coast to coast. So which Packers loss ranks No. 2 on the heartbreaker list?

FOURTH AND 26

In 2003, the Packers appeared to be a team of destiny. That year, Brett Favre turned in the most memorable regular-season performance of his career on Monday Night

Football, the day after his father, Irv, passed away, as the Packers crushed the Raiders 41–7. Packers fans mourned with Favre for the loss of his father, and yet many took it as a sign of divine intervention anytime the Green and Gold caught a break. Late in the season, fans wearing T-shirts with the slogan "In Irv We Trust" were commonplace. And after Al Harris intercepted Seattle quarterback Matt Hasselbeck and ran straight to the north end zone at Lambeau Field to win the NFC Wild Card Game, who was going to argue?

The date: January 11, 2004. The place: Lincoln Financial Field in Philadelphia. The Packers were one play away from upsetting the Eagles in the divisional round of the playoffs. Green Bay had chance after chance to put the game away. In the first half, Ahman Green was stuffed on fourth and goal from the Eagles' 1-yard line. Then, late in the game, on fourth and 1, the Packers elected to punt rather than go for it when a first down would have ended the game. The Eagles had new life. However, the inspired Packers defense pushed Philadelphia backward, and the home team faced fourth and 26 from their own 26-yard line. Freddie Mitchell somehow, some way, found a seam in the Packers' defense, and Donovan McNabb hit him for a 28-yard completion with a minute remaining. It set up a game-tying field goal sending the game into overtime. After a Brett Favre interception, David Akers ended the Packers' season with another field goal and turned the down and distance of "Fourth and 26" into a phrase that will live in infamy for Packers fans.

THE 2008 NFC CHAMPIONSHIP GAME

Everything was falling into place for Packers fans in early 2008. Brett Favre turned back the clock in what turned out to be his final season in green and gold. Head Coach Mike McCarthy led Green Bay to 13 wins, which tied a team record. The Packers beat the Seahawks in the divisional round of the NFC playoffs in what would be known as the "Snow Globe" game. Then the top-seeded Cowboys were upset by the Giants, so the NFC Championship Game would be played at night in mid-January in Green Bay, Wisconsin.

The odds-makers agreed this game was only a formality. The Packers were favored by a touchdown and would easily waltz their way to a win over New York and return to the Super Bowl for the first time in 10 years. However, the Giants had other plans. Even though the game-time temperature was −1°F (a −23°F wind chill), New York quarterback Eli Manning threw the ball early and often to his big wideout, Plaxico Burress, who caught 7 of his 11 passes in the first half and finished the game with 154 receiving yards. The Giants had two chances to win the game in the fourth quarter, but kicker Lawrence Tynes missed two field goals—the second a chip shot from 36 yards out with no time left in regulation. But in overtime, as he did against Philadelphia, Favre threw a costly interception, and the opposition capitalized. Tynes connected from 47 yards out to crush the Super Bowl dreams of Brett Favre and Packers fans.

THE VERDICT

Even though the 2003 Packers loss to the Eagles was gut-wrenching, the loss to the Giants in the NFC Championship Game was more heartbreaking. There was much more on the line for Green Bay against New York. A win would have sent the Packers back to the Super Bowl. Plus, they were at Lambeau Field—a place where they were unbeatable for years—playing the fifth-seeded Giants. The Giants would go on to upset the heavily favored Patriots, whose only loss that year was in Super Bowl XLII. A month later, Brett Favre would retire for the first time, making the long, snowy winter of 2008 the longest off-season in history for Packers fans.

WHO'S THE PACKERS' BIGGEST RIVAL, VIKINGS OR BEARS?

14 Who is the Packers' biggest rival? Is it the Chicago Bears or the Minnesota Vikings? The answer to this debate depends on who you ask. If you ask your parents or grandparents, they would most likely reply the Bears. If you ask your brother, sister, or work colleague, they would answer the Minnesota Vikings. It's a generational thing.

The Packers play each team twice a year, but they have more history with the Bears. The first meeting between the two franchises was in 1921, when the Bears were known as the Decatur Staleys. The names from the old days evoke classic black-and-white snapshots: George "Papa Bear" Halas, Dick Butkus, Gayle Sayers, Sid Luckman and Red Grange. Later on, it was Walter Payton, Jim McMahon, Richard Dent and Brian Urlacher carrying the torch. The two teams combine for 46 members of the Pro Football Hall of Fame. They rank first and second in that category—the Bears with 26, and the Packers with 21.

There are classic episodes between the Packers and Bears: Packers kicker Chester Marcol shocking the Bears by running a blocked field goal into the end zone on opening day in 1980; Charles Martin throwing Jim McMahon to the turf; the instant-replay game; Mike Ditka and Forrest Gregg going at each other first as players and then as coaches. Twice a year, these two teams would throw records out the window and play their biggest games of the year against their most hated rivals. They were the Yankees and Red Sox of pro football.

However, this rivalry lost some of its luster during the Brett Favre era. The Packers won 10 straight meetings against the Bears in the 1990's and then ripped off another seven-game winning streak just after the turn of the century. It's tough to build a rivalry when you already know the outcome before kickoff. Favre simply owned the Bears, beating Chicago 22 times in his Packers career. Favre turned the tide in the Packers-Bears rivalry since Chicago won 12 of 14 meetings in the seven years prior to Favre's arrival in Green Bay.

When the NFL granted Minnesota an expansion team in 1960, the Packers and Bears had already played each other 83 times. Minnesota was Packers territory. And yet, that added spice to an instant rivalry which grew very quickly. The Hamm's Brewing Company in St. Paul was one of the Packers' sponsors, but that changed after the Vikings entered the league. Some football fans in Minnesota converted to the new local team, but some did not.

While the Packers were consistently beating the Bears in the 90's, the Vikings--Packers rivalry grew some roots. The Vikings had some terrific teams in the 1970's, appearing in four Super Bowls (and losing all four), but the rivalry between the Packers and Vikings didn't blossom until the Favre years in the 1990s, when both teams were powers. The games have been so good, the memorable ones have names. For example, there was the T.J. Rubley game. Rubley, a back-up quarterback filling in for the injured Brett Favre, called an ill-fated audible that resulted in an interception that cost the Packers the game at the Metrodome. In the Chris Hovan game, the Vikings' big defensive tackle had to be restrained by teammates while flipping the bird at Brett Favre. Who could forget Randy Moss mooning the crowd after scoring another touchdown in the wild-card playoff game in January of 2005? Antonio Freeman's "Improbable Bobble," creating a Monday night miracle in the rain in 2000, was against the Vikings. You can still hear Al Michaels say, "He did what?" On that same play, Packers Radio Network analyst Larry McCarren proclaimed, "It was meant to be!"

Throughout the years, players have changed sides, adding some fuel to the fire. Darren Sharper, one of the all-time great sound bites, changed his jersey color from green to purple, as did kicker Ryan Longwell. The Packers were interested in interviewing Brad Childress as head coach before Mike McCarthy was hired. However,

Childress never made it out of Minneapolis after interviewing with the Vikings.

And of course, there's Brett Favre. The Packers accused the Vikings of tampering during the Brett Favre soap opera in the Summer of 2008. There were multiple phone calls and text messages between Favre and Vikings offensive coordinator Darrell Bevell, but the NFL eventually ruled that the communication was not out of the ordinary. (That's the same Darrell Bevell that not only led the Badgers to their first Rose Bowl win in 1994, but also cut his teeth as an NFL assistant coach in Green Bay.) The mere thought of seeing Brett Favre dressed in purple has added more intensity to this rivalry.

Aaron Rodgers made his first NFL start on a Monday night in 2008, beating the Vikings in Green Bay and helping Packers fans take that first step in placing Brett Favre in their rearview mirrors. What makes this rivalry so terrific is that both teams have been so good for so long. Before Mike McCarthy and Brad Childress were hired, the series was even at 44 wins apiece.

The Mississippi River separates Wisconsin from Minnesota, but the rivalry knows no territorial boundaries—that's what makes it unique. Like players fraternizing with one another, Packers and Vikings fans are more likely to get along every day except game day. The fans' passion adds to the rivalry. It seems that Bears fans are more fair-weather, while Packers and Vikings fans root for their

57

team no matter what. What do the players think? Consider this. Just days before making his first NFL start against the Vikings, Packers quarterback Aaron Rodgers said, "In the fans' eyes, there's no doubt the Vikings are the Packers' biggest rival."

WHO MAKES THE PACKERS' ALL-TIME TEAM?

15 | HEAD COACH

Without Curly Lambeau, there would be no Green Bay Packers. Without Vince Lombardi, it would be tough to call Green Bay Titletown. Who was the better coach? The answer seems obvious. After all, the biggest prize in pro football is the Lombardi Trophy, given to the Super Bowl champion—but let's not forget about Curly Lambeau.

Lambeau founded the Packers in 1919 and was the team's only coach for its first 30 years. Lambeau was first a player/coach and played halfback for the team from 1919 to 1929. He led the Packers to six championships and is the only Packers coach to win more than 200 games. In fact, his 229 total victories (209 with the Packers) ranks fourth on the NFL all-time wins list.

Lombardi coached the Packers from 1959 to 1967 and won five NFL titles in seven years—a run like no other in NFL history. He's the only coach to lead an NFL team to three straight titles, which included winning the first two Super Bowls. Lombardi went 9–1 in the postseason, losing his first playoff game and winning the final nine. He finished with a 98–30–4 record, good enough for a winning percentage of .758.

Both Lambeau and Lombardi have statues standing side by side in front of the Lambeau Field Atrium. Lambeau is pointing, Lombardi standing. If Lombardi's statue stands a tad taller, it should. He's the all-time coach for football's all-time team. Lombardi's five titles in seven seasons will never be matched. Lambeau stockpiled his numbers during an era which saw as few as nine teams in the league, meaning winning a championship was easier simply because there was less competition. Plus, Lambeau never had to win a playoff game, since the league awarded the championship to the team with the best regular-season record. Lombardi was the master motivator who could get any team up for any game. Both are enshrined in Canton—Lambeau in 1963, and Lombardi in 1971—but it's Lombardi who gets the vote as best coach in Packers history.

16 QUARTERBACK

This is a two-man, Hall of Fame debate. Bart Starr or Brett Favre? You can't go wrong either way but if we are talking the best quarterback in franchise history, number 4 is No. 1. A few pages earlier, you read an entry taking Starr over Favre in a one-game scenario. However, if we are talking about a body of work—production, durability, and longevity—then Favre is the guy.

The numbers are not even close. Favre's numbers given here are just during his time with the Packers. Touchdowns? Favre 442, Starr 152. Yards? Favre 61,655, Starr 24,718. Completions? Favre 5,377, Star 1,808. MVP Awards? Favre 3, Starr 1. It's tough to argue with those numbers.

Favre's most amazing record was his consecutive-starts streak. Favre's first start for the Packers came on September 27 , 1992, in a win against the Pittsburgh Steelers. After he came off the bench a week prior to beat the Bengals with his TD pass to Kitrick Taylor with 13 seconds left, Favre started the next 253 games for the Packers—275 including playoffs. It's just mind-boggling that a man playing the NFL's toughest, most demanding position could take hit after hit and stay healthy enough to play that long. During his streak, Favre had 17 different backups. Around the league, 212 different quarterbacks started at least one game during Favre's streak as a Packer.

Favre also brought charisma to the position along with toughness. He wore his emotions on his sleeve at times, and fans marveled at his boyish enthusiasm. Almost every week, he would give us a "Favre" moment, a play that made you gasp. It wasn't always a good gasp, either; Favre threw 288 interceptions while he was a Packer and holds the NFL record in that department, as well. That was the beauty of Favre—fans had to take the good with the bad. It was a roller coaster at times, but it was a fun ride. Favre rallied the Packers 40 different times for victories in

61

the fourth quarter. Think about that for a moment. In two and a half *seasons'* worth of games, Favre brought his team back from a fourth-quarter deficit or broke a tie.

This is not to knock Bart Starr. He was a fantastic quarterback and one of the biggest winners of all time. Starr was the NFL MVP in 1966 and led the league in passing three times. He led the Packers to six division titles and five world championships, including two Super Bowl wins in which he earned the MVP Award. He wasn't considered a "gunslinger" like Favre, but Starr could make the passes he needed to make and was a perfect quarterback for Vince Lombardi's Packers.

Choosing between these two great quarterbacks is like trying to figure out if you would rather order vanilla ice cream (Starr) or rocky road (Favre). Starr was one of the first "game managers," while Favre was the difference-maker, week in and week out, good or bad. More times than not, the rocky road was sweet for Favre and the Packers. Favre is the greatest quarterback in Packers history.

17 TAILBACK

Although the franchise is defined by quarterbacks, there's no doubt that running the football in Green Bay is crucial to the Packers' success, especially late in the season when winter's arrival makes it tough to rely on the passing game. When choosing the best tailback in Packers history, two names rise to the top of the list: Tony Canadeo and Paul Hornung. Canadeo has his number 3 retired, while four players, including quarterback Vince Ferragamo have been issued Hornung's number 5. However, this is one instance where the guy whose number has been retired is second-best.

There's no doubt Canadeo was a groundbreaking running back. He was the first Packer and third player in NFL history to rush for more than 1,000 yards in a single season. And Canadeo was more than just a guy who ran the football. He gained 8,667 all-purpose yards in his career. He led the Packers in passing for a season, started out as a defensive back who finished with nine career interceptions and even punted 45 different times as a pro. Canadeo was inducted into the Pro Football Hall of Fame in 1974 and is very much deserving of the honor. However, there was a better tailback for the Packers.

Paul Hornung was the face of the franchise when the 1950s turned into the 1960s. "The Golden Boy" won the Heisman Trophy at Notre Dame and carried his success to Green Bay. Also a man with a golden toe, Hornung kicked and ran his way to the NFL scoring title for three consecutive seasons, from 1959 to 1961. His NFL-record 176 points in 1960 stood the test of time for 46 years before San Diego's LaDainian Tomlinson broke the record in 2006. Hornung was not only a favorite of Vince Lombardi, he was *the* favorite of the legendary coach. Lombardi treated Hornung as a son. Even his one-year NFL suspension for gambling in 1963 did little to tarnish his golden image with the no-nonsense coach. Hornung managed to survive the suspension and returned to the Packers for three more seasons, helping them win two more titles. In all, Hornung played for four championship teams in Green Bay.

You can look at the numbers—Canadeo actually had more rushing yards than Hornung, 4,197 to 3,711. However, Hornung was the more dominant player of his era. He was the NFL MVP in 1961 and scored an NFL-record 19 points in the Packers' 37–0 shutout of the New York Giants in the NFL Championship Game. Technically, it was a game that Hornung should never have played in. After he had been summoned into the service by the Army, it took a call from Lombardi to President John F. Kennedy to get Hornung a leave to play in the 1961 title game. An ardent football fan, Kennedy said the country deserved to see the two best teams battle for the title, and Hornung made the most of his leave.

But it was more than just numbers for Hornung. He was a guy that women loved and men wanted to emulate. He had panache, or as the kids say these days, he had swagger. Parents named their sons Paul in the 1960s—granted, some were named after a member of the Beatles—but many were named after "the Golden Boy." He was the most versatile back of his era and was inducted into the Pro Football Hall of Fame in 1986. Paul Hornung is the best back in Packers history, and he should have his number 5 retired.

18 FULLBACK

Most Packers fans know the name Clarke Hinkle but not the player. When the modern-day Packers practice on the field west of the Don Hutson Center, they are practicing on Clarke Hinkle Field. Hinkle was a standout two-way player who terrorized opponents from 1932 to 1941. He could do it all—he was a fullback who could block, catch, and even handle the kicking duties. Plus, he was a bruising linebacker when playing both offense and defense was the norm. Hinkle was named All-Pro four times in his career and is well-deserving of his placement in the Pro Football Hall of Fame. However, if this is an argument on who was the best fullback, Jim Taylor's the choice.

Taylor is the Packers all-time leading rusher, with 8,207 yards in his nine seasons in Green Bay. Hinkle ended his career with 3,860. Both players led the Packers in rushing for seven seasons. Taylor rushed for 1,000 yards in seven consecutive seasons—a team record. Hinkle's best year was 1937, when he gained 552 yards. Comparing players in different eras is almost impossible—therefore, relying on statistics is one way to make an assessment. Offenses were far less sophisticated in Hinkle's day; however, he never led the NFL in rushing. Taylor led the league in 1962 and was second in four other seasons. Taylor was the premier back in the league in his prime. He sits atop most of the Packers' individual rushing records, even

65

though he retired more than four decades ago. Taylor's 19 touchdowns in 1962 is still the club record. He scored four touchdowns in a game three separates times, also a team best. His 81 career scores blow away second-place Ahman Green, who scored 53 touchdowns in Green Bay.

Jim Taylor rushed for more than 100 yards in 26 games in his nine seasons. More importantly, he was half of a dynamic running duo with Paul Hornung. When you look at the numbers, it was Taylor and not Hornung who led the Packers in rushing on the way to winning the four NFL championships that the two were a part of. Taylor was named to the Pro Bowl five times in his career and was elected to the Pro Football Hall of Fame in 1976. Jim Taylor was not only the best fullback in Packers history; Some argue that he was the best pure running back, period.

WIDE RECEIVER

Seventeen minutes. Seventeen minutes made the difference between Donald Montgomery Hutson wearing a Packers uniform and Brooklyn Dodgers gear. To think that he was minutes away from never playing in Green Bay! In 1935—before there was an NFL draft—Hutson signed contracts to play for both the Green Bay Packers and the NFL's Brooklyn Dodgers. The Alabama star sent both contracts to the NFL and let league president Joe Carr decide his fate. Since the Packers contract was postmarked 17 minutes earlier than the Dodgers contract, Hutson was awarded to the Packers. There's really not much of an argument here—Hutson is the best wide receiver in franchise history.

Hutson is credited for inventing and developing the modern-day pass pattern. His numbers are mind-boggling. He played 11 seasons with the Packers at a time when passing was a rarity and yet still scored 99 touchdowns. In fact, over a three-year span in the prime of his career, Hutson scored 38 receiving touchdowns from 1941 to 1943, when the NFL played just 11 regular-season games a year. Hutson played both ways, as well, and over those three seasons, he picked off 16 passes and returned one for a touchdown. He also scored two rushing touchdowns in 1941. Hutson handled the placekicking duties for the Packers and owns the NFL record for scoring 29 points in a single quarter (four touchdowns, five extra points) against the Lions in 1945. His finest season was 1942, when he caught 74 passes for 1,211 yards, scored 17 touchdowns, and kicked 33 extra points and a field goal.

Hutson was a burner—he was once clocked under 10 seconds in the 100-yard dash, a world-class time in any era, but especially in the late 1930s when Jesse Owens held the world record running 100 meters in 10.2 seconds. Granted, 100 meters equals 110 yards but Hutson running a sub-10 second 100-yard dash was still impressive. He led the NFL in touchdowns nine times, in receptions eight times, in receiving yards seven times, and in scoring for five straight seasons. He was a consensus All-Pro five times and a member of three teams that won the NFL championship (1936, 1939, and 1944). More than six decades after his retirement, Don Hutson still holds 10 NFL records. Packers team historian Lee Remmel calls Hutson the greatest player in team history. Even the modern-day Packers are blown away by Hutson's achievements. When asked who he thought was the best wideout in Packers history, Donald Driver said without hesitation, "Gotta go with Don Hutson—no doubt."

So who's No. 2? "Hutson one, Sterling Sharpe two, James Lofton three," Driver said. When it's all said and done, Driver will be in this conversation, and perhaps even Greg Jennings will, but for now, it's Sharpe versus Lofton. Lofton is in the Hall of Fame. Sharpe is not, although, many believe Sharpe's prickly attitude toward the media has cost him some votes for that honor. He'd be a shoo-in were it not for an injury to his spine that cut his career short, forcing him to retire after just seven seasons with Green Bay. Lofton holds the Packers record with 9,656 receiving yards, and he's third to Sharpe and now Driver in receptions with 530. Sharpe caught 112 passes in 1993 and 108 in 1992, which are the top two season totals in Packers history. Lofton made seven Pro Bowls with the Packers; Sharpe made it to Hawaii five times.

Lofton was more likely to burn you deep, while you could always count on Sharpe to come down with the clutch catch. If it wasn't for Sharpe's injury you could make a little stronger case for him, but you can't argue with Lofton's longevity. Lofton became the first post–Lombardi era Packer to enter the Pro Football Hall of Fame in 2003 and he's the choice as second-best wide receiver in Packers history.

TIGHT END

Who is the best tight end in Packers history, Mark Chmura, Ron Kramer, or Paul Coffman? Remember, this is strictly a football debate. Yes, Mark Chmura was involved in a highly publicized scandal and subsequent court case after his playing career ended, but this argument is about his playing career only.

Kramer and Chmura have similar numbers. Both played seven seasons with the Packers, and both played in 89 games. Chmura holds the edge in catches, 188 to 170, but Kramer gained more yards, 2,594 to Chmura's 2,253. Kramer had the better average yards per catch of 15.3 to Chmura's average of 12 yards per catch. Chmura scored more touchdowns than Kramer, 17 to 15. Kramer played his final three seasons in Detroit, while Chmura retired after seven seasons because of a neck injury. Chmura was named to the Pro Bowl three times and was an All-Pro once. Kramer made the Pro Bowl in 1962 and was a two-time All-Pro. Both players helped the Packers win NFL championships. Both were considered solid, if not above-average, blockers. Kramer entered the Packers Hall of Fame in 1975, while Chmura should get serious consideration. But don't waste your time flipping a coin between these two guys, since they are both battling for second-best.

Paul Coffman arrived in Green Bay as an undrafted free agent in the summer of 1978. He begged for a tryout before the draft and impressed the coaches enough to earn an invitation back for training camp. Coffman made the team but did not play a single snap. However, he enjoyed a breakout season in 1979, leading the Packers in receptions with 56, which broke Ron Kramer's team record. Coffman had two more catches that season than future Hall of Famer James Lofton.

Coffman was elected to the Pro Bowl three times during his eight seasons in Green Bay. He finished his career with 322 receptions for 4,223 yards, and he scored 39 touchdowns. Coffman was also a key player in one of the greatest regular-season games in Packers history. On Monday, October 17, 1983, the Packers beat the Redskins 48–47 under the lights at Lambeau Field in the highest-scoring game in the history of Monday Night Football. Coffman caught six passes that night for 124 yards and two touchdowns. Coffman's Packers teams never won a Super Bowl and never won an NFC Central title, but it wasn't because of Coffman. He was consistent. Aside from the strike year of 1982, Coffman caught at least 40 passes each year from 1979 to 1985. Will we even let it slide that Coffman finished his career with the Minnesota Vikings? Yes. He was too good for too long. Paul Coffman is the best tight end in Packers history.

21 TACKLE

The only player to even give Forrest Gregg a sniff of competition at offensive tackle would be Robert "Cal" Hubbard. During Hubbard's era, he stood head and shoulders above the competition. At 6'5" and 250 pounds, Hubbard was a giant during his playing days from 1929 to 1933 and in 1935. Hubbard played tackle on both sides of the ball and is well-deserving of his spot in the Hall of Fame, but he is another example of an outstanding player forgotten by most modern football fans. Hubbard was one of the earliest offensive linemen who had the rare combination of size and speed. An interesting side note about Hubbard—after he retired from pro football, he became a full-time baseball umpire and eventually worked American League games. Hubbard is the only man to be enshrined in both the Pro Football and Baseball Halls of Fame.

If you need any convincing that Forrest Gregg is the best offensive tackle in Packers history, consider that Vince Lombardi called Gregg "the finest player I have ever coached." How's that for an endorsement? Gregg made the Pro Bowl nine times and was named an All-Pro eight times during his career.

Gregg was considered undersized, standing 6'4'' and 240 pounds, but what he lacked in size, he more than made up for with his brains. He was a pioneer of film study, watching countless hours a week to prepare for an upcoming opponent. Gregg spent so much time watching film that he could predict every move from an opponent, making him seem even quicker. He was smart, he was tough, he was durable, and he was reliable. Gregg was the Packers' iron man before Brett Favre, having played 187 consecutive games. The only knock on Gregg was that he was unable to walk away from the game. He retired four times and came back to play on three separate occasions.

Gregg was a much better player for the Packers then a head coach. His four-year record walking the sidelines from 1984 to 1987 was just 25–37–1. However, he was the premier offensive tackle of his day and the best in Packers history.

22 GUARD

The Packers organization claims 21 members in the Pro Football Hall of Fame. Only one of the 21 played offensive guard—Mike Michalske. He was a two-way player from 1929 to 1935, and 1937, as well. However, calling Michalske the best guard in Packers history is a stretch, since the game was completely different during the Great Depression. That leaves us with Jerry Kramer, Fred "Fuzzy" Thurston, and Gale Gillingham.

All three are members of the Packers Hall of Fame, but all three are on the outside of the Pro Football Hall of Fame, looking in. Still, all three were tremendous offensive guards. The tandem of Kramer and Thurston defined the Packers' "power sweep" of the Lombardi era. They were nicknamed "the Guardian Angels," since they were the key to the basic running play in Lombardi's offense. The guards would pull or lead the running back around the end, clearing a path for him to run. Kramer's and Thurston's roles were imperative for the success of the power sweep.

Kramer is probably best known for his block in the Ice Bowl, the 1967 NFL Championship Game, where he and center Ken Bowman cleared the way for Bart Starr to lunge for the winning score against the Cowboys in the closing seconds of the game. Kramer was a six-time All-Pro and made three Pro Bowls. Thurston was an All-Pro five times, and in 1962, he received more votes for All-Pro than any player in the league. It's fitting that we talk of Thurston and Kramer together, since they were the mainstays on the offensive line during the Lombardi dynasty. The two even entered the Packers Hall of Fame in the same class of 1975. However, the two were mentioned together so often that it's tough to differentiate between them.

It was Gale Gillingham who replaced Thurston in the starting lineup for the final two regular-season games in 1966 and then permanently in 1967. He was a natural at the position. We hear so often about the undersized player with the big heart and real determination under Lombardi. However, Gillingham was the exception. At 280 pounds, he was about 20 pounds heavier than the average offensive guard of his era, yet he could still run with any lineman. He went to five Pro Bowls and was named an All-Pro for three straight seasons, from 1969 to 1971. But in 1972, Head Coach Dan Devine did something inexplicable—he moved Gillingham to the defensive line. As a team captain, Gillingham went along with the foolish move. In his second game as a defensive tackle, he suffered a season-ending knee injury. Gillingham moved back to his natural position the next season and played at a All-Pro level that season and the next, but he was never again the same player. If you ask any of the older Packers, they'll agree that Gillingham, in his prime, was the most dominant and gifted offensive lineman of the Lombardi era. He could do it all. If it wasn't for the knee injury, we could very well be talking about Pro Football Hall of Famer Gale Gillingham. In any case, we can still call him the greatest guard in Packers history.

CENTER

Offensive linemen are the unsung heroes of pro football. Even though every play starts with the snap most football fans have trouble naming the guy snapping. Who's Charlie Brock, you ask? Even the most die-hard Packers fan may have trouble coming up with Brock's bio. Brock was one of Curly Lambeau's best offensive linemen during the 1940s, and he was named to the Packers' first All-Time team, spanning the franchise's first 25 years. Brock helped the Packers to two NFL championships in 1939 and 1944. He was named to the Pro Bowl three times—second-most of any center in Packers history next to Jim Ringo.

It's a shame that Jim Ringo's name is always linked to his well-documented departure from Green Bay. As legend has it, Ringo and his agent asked Vince Lombardi for a hefty raise in 1964 after Ringo had played in seven Pro Bowls for the Packers. Lombardi was insulted that a player would bring an agent into his office to negotiate. He excused himself and came back moments later to tell Ringo and his representation that they were talking to the wrong guy on the wrong team, since the center would now be snapping for the Philadelphia Eagles. It's a terrific story that Lombardi never went out of his way to correct. However, it never happened. Ringo did not have an agent at that time, which was commonplace among athletes of the 1960s. Before his death, Ringo told Rob Reischel of the *Milwaukee Journal-Sentinel,* "I didn't have an agent...I really don't know how that story got going. Sometimes people create their own stories." The trade turned out to be a blessing for Ringo, whose family already lived in

Pennsylvania, and it allowed the center to finish out his Hall of Fame career with the Eagles.

There's no debating Ringo's playing ability. Like many of his teammates during the Lombardi era, Jim Ringo was undersized but made up for it with tenacity and determination. Before he was traded to the Eagles in 1964, Ringo started 126 consecutive games for the Packers and was the starting point on the Packers' "power sweep," the running play that defined Lombardi's offense. Ringo helped the Packers win back-to-back NFL championships in 1961 and 1962 and was named an All-Pro seven times with Green Bay—eight times overall. Five times in Green Bay, Ringo was a consensus All-Pro, an honor matched by just one other Packer, the incomparable Don Hutson—arguably the best wide receiver in NFL history. Ringo was inducted into the Packers Hall of Fame in 1974 and the Pro Football Hall of Fame in 1981. Jim Ringo was the best center in Packers history.

24 KICKER

The Packers kicking records are represented with some legendary names: Curly Lambeau, Don Hutson, Paul Hornung, and Jerry Kramer all booted field goals and extra points for the Packers. All kicked before specialists turned the kicker into the most valuable scorers on the team. They will all be left out of this argument. Jan Stenerud is the only full-time kicker in the Pro Football Hall of Fame. Even though he spent the latter years of his career in Green Bay (1980–1983), most football fans consider Stenerud a member of the Kansas City Chiefs. So Stenerud is not part of this argument. That leaves Chester Marcol, Chris Jacke, and Ryan Longwell in contention for the title of best kicker in Packers history.

Chester Marcol solidified a position that gave Packers fans headaches for years. From 1968 to 1971, the Packers used Mike Mercer, Jerry Kramer, Chuck Mercein, Erroll Mann, Booth Lusteg, Dale Livingston, Lou Michaels, Tim Webster, and Dave Conway as placekickers. Nine different kickers scored points for the Packers in four seasons. Chester Marcol changed that. Marcol's rookie season in 1972 was a big reason why the Packers won 10 games and the NFC Central title. Marcol led the NFL in scoring with 128 points, was named an All-Pro, and was the league's Rookie of the Year. Packers fans loved him for his ability to torture the Chicago Bears. Not only did Marcol's five field goals help the Packers sweep the Bears in 1972, he also beat Chicago with a field goal with 13 seconds left in a preseason game. His ability to stick it to the Bears moved Bears head coach Abe Gibron to call him "the Polish Prince." The nickname stuck.

In the season opener in 1980, Marcol scored the biggest points of his career using two feet not one. His potential game-winning field goal in overtime against the hated Bears was blocked by Chicago defensive tackle Alan Page. The ball bounced right back to Marcol, who scampered into the end zone for the winning score. It would be the final chapter of a playing career in Green Bay that lasted nine seasons. He made the Pro Bowl twice (1972 and 1974) and was a consensus All-Pro in 1972—an honor no other Packers kicker can claim.

Chris Jacke ranks third on the Packers all-time scoring list and is just a field goal behind second-place Don Hutson. He never made it to Hawaii as a Pro Bowler, but in 1993, he was honored on the Associated Press All-Pro team. Jacke converted 72 percent of his field goals in his eight seasons and missed just five extra points in 306 career attempts. Jacke helped the Packers get to the Super Bowl, thanks to a 114-point season in 1996, and he also made two field goals in Super Bowl XXXI against the Patriots.

Ryan Longwell took consistency to a new level when Jacke was let go after the 1996 season. Longwell faced an uphill battle at training camp in 1997. He was a free agent competing against a third-round draft pick in Brett Conway. A tired leg sent Conway to the training room, and Longwell made the most of his opportunity, winning the job and keeping it for nine seasons. Longwell played in 114 games as a Packer and scored in every single contest. He scored more points than any Packer in franchise history, and he led the Packers in scoring for nine straight seasons—also a team record. He made 81 percent of his field goal attempts and 99 percent of his extra points. Like Jacke, Longwell never made the Pro Bowl as a Packer, but he was named to the *Football Digest* All-Pro team in 2003 and 2004.

Put the kickers in two separate categories because of their eras. Ryan Longwell's numbers with the Packers are simply better than Chris Jacke's. Longwell was more consistent and kicked longer—he has more field goals made (226) than Jacke attempted (224)—so the contest is between Longwell and Marcol. Even though Marcol made just 61.5 percent of his field goals as a Packer, he was considered the best kicker in the NFL for two separate seasons. However, you cannot beat Longwell's statistics. Longwell scored more than 100 points in his first eight seasons in Green Bay. Granted, teams kick more field goals in this day and age, but Longwell's consistency would impress in any era. At one point, he held the NFL record as the most accurate kicker of all time. He still ranks in the top 15—remarkable when you consider that the NFL changed its policy in 1999 and introduced a "K" ball used only for kicks, which made it harder for kickers to perform. The only negative for Longwell is that he left Green Bay to play for the Vikings for better money. In the end, the slam dunk for this argument comes from longtime Packers beat writer for the *Milwaukee Journal-Sentinel,* Bob McGinn, who is one of the most respected football writers in the country. When Longwell left Green Bay and signed with Minnesota as a free agent, McGinn called him "the greatest kicker in Green Bay Packers history." McGinn's word is gold, and Longwell is the choice. End of argument.

25 DEFENSIVE END

A dynamic defensive end is a game changer in the NFL. He's someone who can stuff a run and crush a quarterback. Some teams have never had such a player. The Packers have two. This is a win-win. You can't go wrong either way—Willie Davis or Reggie White. They are two of the best defensive ends to ever play professional football. Willie Davis helped Vince Lombardi win five championships and was the model of consistency. He never missed a game, playing all 162 games in his career; however, his Packers career (1960–1969) was before the NFL kept official sack or tackle totals. John Turney, a statistician with the Professional Football Researchers' Association, reported that Davis would have had at least 100 sacks in his career, including at least 40 in a three-year span from 1963 to 1965.

The NFL did keep track of fumble recoveries during the 1960s, and Davis had 21—more than anyone in Packers history. Credit Lombardi for plucking Davis away from the Cleveland Browns and turning him into a defensive end. The legendary coach was enthralled with the big man. Lombardi said there were three components which made a great lineman: size, speed and agility. At 6'3" and 245, Davis possessed all three. Davis was named an All-Pro five times, played in five Pro Bowls, and entered the Pro Football Hall of Fame in 1981. But, as great as Davis was, there's no one who can hold a candle to Reggie White.

Fans absolutely loved Reggie White. He was a larger-than-life figure, the type of player even non-football fans watched and admired. The chant *"Reg-gie! Reg-gie! Reg-gie!"* is one of the best chants in the history of Lambeau Field. "The Minister of Defense" was the most feared defensive end of his era. He finished his six-year Packers career as the team's all-time sack leader with 68.5 (since passed by Kabeer Gbaja-Biamilla).

But it was more than just statistics with Reggie White. He was the type of player that made everyone around him better—no one would dare disappoint the team's defensive leader. White arrived in Green Bay as the biggest free agent signing in NFL history, and he was worth every penny. He helped the Packers defense jump from 23rd in total defense the year before he came to town to No. 2 in his first season. White terrorized opposing quarterbacks and offensive linemen. He sacked Drew Bledsoe a record three times in Super Bowl XXXI. His 198 career sacks rank him second behind Bruce Smith on the NFL's all-time list. In his career, White sacked 75 different quarterbacks. The guy who was dropped the most? Phil Simms, sacked 15 times by White.

It's tough to compare players of different eras, but most would agree that as great as Willie Davis was in his day,

Reggie White was better. White was a guy who lifted a team, showing the right way to be a professional. He was a spiritual leader, an ordained minister, who popularized the post-game prayer at midfield. He was a guy who credits God with healing his multitude of injuries during his playing career. He was certainly a special player with unequaled talent, and his intensity was unmatched. White remains the only player in football history to have three jerseys retired in the same season by three different teams (the Packers, the Eagles, and the University of Tennessee).

White was a proud man who hated losing. Those on the sidelines as the Packers lost to the Cowboys in the NFC Championship game in January of 1996 can attest that Reggie would not be the subject of any pictures or video capturing the agony of defeat. White stormed toward camera operators yelling, "Get that camera off me! Turn that camera off!" Who was going to argue with the Minister of Defense? That exemplified Reggie White's intensity. In the midst of defeat, he was a man who did not want the world to see his efforts on the field go unrewarded. Reggie was livid. He came up one game short of playing in the Super Bowl. His pride was hurt and he did not want the cameras capturing the moment. That was who he was, a man who wore his emotions on his sleeve. Reggie had a burning desire to win which made the next season, 1996, so special. White led the NFL's top-ranked defense to the Packers' first championship in 29 years.

Reggie made it cool to win, cool to pray, and cool to believe. He made 13 straight Pro Bowls and entered the Pro Football Hall of Fame on the first ballot posthumously in 2006. It seems obvious, but Reggie White is the best defensive end in Packers history.

26 DEFENSIVE TACKLE

If loyalty and longevity were the sole criteria, Dave Hanner would win any argument about the best defensive tackle for the Packers. Hanner spent 44 years with the Green Bay Packers as a player, coach, and scout. Known as "Hawg," Hanner anchored the defensive line from 1952 to 1964. He made it to the Pro Bowl twice, in 1953 and 1954, which is even more impressive when you consider the Packers won just six games in those two seasons combined. Hanner was good but played alongside a great defensive tackle—a man he would later coach: Henry Jordan.

Jordan was a cornerstone in the building blocks of Vince Lombardi's dynasty. The shrewd Lombardi obtained him for a fourth-round draft pick in 1959. Considered undersized at 6'2" and 248 pounds, Jordan won battles with his smarts and quickness. He was named as an All-Pro five times (1960–1964) and played in four Pro Bowls.

Jordan might get lost in the shuffle with all the greats who played for Lombardi—after all, eleven Lombardi era Packers have been elected to the Hall of Fame. But Jordan was a winner. He played in seven NFL title games, including Super Bowls I and II. And he was durable. He missed just two games over the first 12 years of his career. Jordan was also a personality. He was the guy who, when asked how Lombardi treated his players, said he treated everyone the same—like dogs. Jordan's finest moment may have been in the 1967 Western Conference Championship Game against the Los Angeles Rams, when the defensive tackle registered three and a half sacks in a Packers victory. He was inducted into the Hall of Fame in 1995.

27 LINEBACKER

When you think of a linebacker, what comes to mind? Two words come to mind. Nitschke and Butkus. The names even sound tough. They are simply two of the greatest linebackers from two of the greatest franchises in NFL history. Ray Nitschke and Dick Butkus, with the Packers and the Bears respectively, defined the position. It just so happened that both men played at the University of Illinois. In the NFL, the two would line up on opposite sidelines twice a year every time Green Bay played Chicago. Watching those two proud franchises go toe to toe in the 1960s and early 1970s must have been like watching a linebacker clinic. Forget about Brian Urlacher—Butkus is the Bears' all-time greatest linebacker. Nitschke is the greatest Packer linebacker, hands down. No one even comes close.

Incredibly, Nitschke was named to the Pro Bowl just once. Fred Carr, Dave Robinson, and Bill Forester all went to more Pro Bowls than Nitschke. Early on in the Lombardi era, the Packers had the best linebacker unit in the NFL in Nitschke, Forester, and Dan Currie, but the leader of the pack was Nitschke.

Nitschke's biography lists him as an All-Pro from 1964 to 1966, and he was inducted into the Pro Football Hall of Fame in 1978 and helped the Packers win five championships. But Nitschke was more than that. He was one of those rare football players whose toughness personified his team: Toughness equals Nitschke; Nitschke equals football. If you were growing up in Wisconsin in the late 1960s and had a chip on your shoulder, Ray Nitschke was *the* guy you wanted to be—number 66. The late Dick Schaap once called Nitschke "the toughest and meanest player on the best football team that ever was."

The Green Bay Packers have been around for almost nine decades, and yet they have just six jersey numbers retired. By comparison, the New York Yankees have retired 16 numbers, and the Boston Celtics have retired 20. Of the six numbers the Packers have retired, one of those belongs to Ray Nitschke who terrified offensive players league-wide during his 15 years in the NFL. If the question is, "Who challenges Ray Nitschke?" the answer is, "No one."

SAFETY

Emlen Tunnell and Willie Wood are the two Packers safeties in the Pro Football Hall of Fame. Since Tunnell played most of his career in New York with the Giants, he's left out of this debate. Wood has a serious challenger by a guy who deserves consideration for a spot in Canton: LeRoy Butler. So, who was the better safety, Wood or Butler? The two standout safeties for the Packers combined for 86 interceptions and 12 Pro Bowl appearances. Both men led the Packers in interceptions in five seasons. Willie Wood was named as one of the three safeties on the NFL's All-Decade team for the 1960s. LeRoy Butler was one of the four safeties on the NFL's All-Decade team for the 1990s. These two make for one of the closest battles of any position on this All-Time Packers team.

Butler was the backbone of the NFL's top-ranked defense in 1996, helping the Packers to a victory in Super Bowl XXXI. He was one of the few who could run like a cornerback and hit like a linebacker. Butler finished his 12-year career with 953 tackles, 38 interceptions, and 20.5 sacks. He is also the originator of the "Lambeau Leap." An impressive resume, no question—but Willie Wood tops it.

Wood had to beg to get into the NFL. After going undrafted in 1960, he embarked on a letter-writing campaign before he was invited to join 24 other Packers defensive back hopefuls in Green Bay. Wood made the team and went on to become the greatest safety in team history.

He picked off 48 passes in his 12-year career. He helped the Packers to six NFL Championship Games, winning five, including the first two Super Bowls. It was Wood who intercepted a Len Dawson pass in the third quarter of Super Bowl I to break open a close contest against the AFL champion Kansas City Chiefs. That kind of big-play ability made Wood a star. He made the Pro Bowl eight times, was All-NFL six times, and in 1962 led the NFL with nine interceptions. He was so athletic that in 1961, Wood led the NFL in averaging 16.1 yards per punt return.

Like so many of the Packers listed on this All-Time team, Wood was considered undersized for his position. But like so many of the Packers listed here, Wood made up for his lack of size with grit, determination, and athleticism. He made the most of his 5'10", 160-pound frame. Even though he was considered small for a defensive back, he was durable, playing in 166 straight games—the third-longest streak in Packers history behind Brett Favre and Forrest Gregg. Wood was also tough—so tough that Ray Nitschke once said he was more afraid of Wood than of Vince Lombardi. Wood had eyes of fire and would take out his aggression on his opponents. Like LeRoy Butler, Wood played all 12 of his NFL seasons with the Packers. Wood is one of just seven undrafted free agents to make it to Canton and the Pro Football Hall of Fame. Really, for All-Time safety, both Wood and Butler have incredible resumes, but for this argument, it's Wood by a hair.

29 CORNERBACK

The only serious competition here for Herb Adderley is Willie Buchanon. Perhaps if Charles Woodson had started his career in Green Bay, he might be added to this mix, as well. In reality, this is a one-sided argument for Herb Adderley. Yes, Buchanon was a standout cornerback who picked off 21 passes during his seven seasons in Green Bay and was named to three Pro Bowls before getting traded to San Diego in 1978. Yes, Buchanon still shares the NFL record with four interceptions in one game. But it was Adderley who set the standard for defensive backs, even if he took an unlikely path to get there.

Adderley came to Green Bay as a highly touted running back drafted in the first round in 1961 out of Michigan State. The competition in the backfield was stiff, to say the least. Adderley was battling for playing time with future Hall of Famers Paul Hornung and Jim Taylor. It wasn't until midway through Adderley's rookie season, when starting cornerback Hank Gremminger went down with an injury, that Vince Lombardi switched Adderley to the defensive backfield. Lombardi later mused that his stubbornness to keep Adderley on offensive almost cost him one of the greatest cornerbacks to play the game. Adderley had tremendous instincts and was lightning quick. The speedy corner was a five-time Pro Bowler and a five-time All-Pro. He was the old-school definition of *playmaker* before the word became regularly used in

88

sports vernacular. Adderley scored seven touchdowns on interception returns and still shares the Packers record with three defensive scores in 1965. Adderley's biggest interception came in Lombardi's final game as Packers head coach, in Super Bowl II. The veteran cornerback jumped on a Daryle Lamonica pass and returned it 60 yards to put the game away early in the fourth quarter, helping the Packers to a 33–14 win against the Raiders.

Above all, Adderley was a winner. He won five NFL titles with the Packers and played in four of the first six Super Bowls (two with the Packers, two with the Cowboys). He was inducted into the Pro Football Hall of Fame in 1980. Herb Adderley was the greatest cornerback in Packers history.

30 PUNTER

The position of punter is the weakest and most inconsistent of any on the Packers' All-Time roster. Green Bay has never had a punter make All-Pro or go to the Pro Bowl. Over the last two decades, there's been a revolving door at the punter's position. Seven different men punted regularly in the 1990s. The Packers had six different punters in the first eight years after the turn of the century. No Packers punter has ever led the NFL in punting average. The brutal weather conditions absolutely play a role—however, it's plain to see that the position of punter has not been a strength of the Packers, with the exception of a four-year period in the 1990s.

Craig Hentrich arrived in Green Bay after getting drafted and then cut by the Jets in 1993. Hentrich was stashed on the Packers practice squad in 1993 and then beat out Bryan Wagner for the punting job a year later. Hentrich handled the punter's position for four seasons and left Green Bay as the all-time leader in gross average in a career: 42.8 yards. His best season was 1997, when he averaged 45 yards a punt. Hentrich also handled kickoff duties in the Super Bowl–winning season of 1996.

Speaking of Super Bowl specialists, Don Chandler handled the punting duties for Green Bay in the first Super Bowl as well as the NFL Championship game the year prior. Chandler spent just two seasons as the Packers punter and performed well—he still holds the franchise record for the longest punt in team history, a 90-yarder in 1965—but Chandler's tenure was brief and most Packers fans remember him more for his place-kicking than his punting ability.

There's no questioning Hentrich's legacy, he was a punter with a rocket for a right leg. Former Packers general manager Ron Wolf says one of his biggest regrets was letting Craig Hentrich go during free agency in 1998. The big hang-up was money; Hentrich was on the cusp of becoming the first punter to make more than $1 million a year. Wolf and the Packers said no, and Hentrich then became a Pro Bowler in his first year with the Tennessee Titans. Not less than five years later, seven different punters would top the million-dollar-a-year average. The Packers had four different punters in that five-year span. Meanwhile, Hentrich stabilized the punting position in Nashville for the next decade. The Packers have had some good punters: Josh Bidwell in the early 2000s; Dick Deschaine in the 1950s; Chandler; even Max McGee was a solid punter. But no one was spectacular. Craig Hentrich was the closest one to being truly special and he was allowed to leave Green Bay for greener pastures.

BETTER BLOWUP: SHERMAN AND THE CELL PHONE OR HOLMGREN AND THE FAN?

31 Mike Sherman and Mike Holmgren felt pressure for the same reason—not winning enough football games. Sherman's club in 2005 was 1–6, and Holmgren's team, coming off back-to-back Super Bowl appearances was 7–4 in 1998. Sherman and Holmgren felt enough pressure to take issue with a reporter and a fan respectively, and each lost his cool.

Mike Sherman was midway through his regularly scheduled media briefing when he was interrupted by a ringing phone. Instead of ignoring the annoyance, as he had done in the past, Sherman stopped mid-answer and gave the media a stern lecture. "I don't understand that," Sherman said as he walked away from the podium. "That stuff to me, to be honest with you, is a total lack of respect for each other. Forget me, you don't have to respect me, but respect each other." It was a rare moment of emotion, albeit controlled emotion, from Sherman, who was at the time a spokesman for a Green Bay cell–phone company. Like children wondering who had ticked off Dad, the members of the media looked toward the back of the room, wondering who the guilty party was. No one stepped forward. Sherman's Packers didn't step forward that season, either, finishing 4–12 and costing Sherman his job.

Mike Holmgren was walking off Lambeau Field at half-time of the Packers' game against the Eagles on November 29, 1998. Holmgren's team was winning more than losing that year but not winning enough for a team who was expected to make its third straight trip to the Super Bowl. The speculation was that Holmgren wanted to be a head coach *and* a general manager—something he could not do in Green Bay, since Ron Wolf was the Packers GM. Local Green Bay television stations were videotaping Holmgren's walk off the field when a fan challenged the coach. "C'mon Mike, stop thinking about the next job and get going on this one," the fan said. Holmgren fired back, "(Expletive) you! (Expletive) you!" The head coach gave the fan the finger. Holmgren later apologized, saying the fan verbally attacked his family, although the videotape of the incident proved otherwise.

As far as blowups go, on a scale of 1 to 10, give Sherman a 5 and Holmgren a 10. Anyone who's had a business meeting interrupted by a ringing cell phone can relate with Sherman's reaction. Ringing cell phones during news conferences are a major problem. They are annoying. It's embarrassing and inexcusable. However, there's no excuse for going after a fan, in one's home stadium, no less. A fan has every right to boo or question a coach, as long as he or she doesn't use profanity. Holmgren's behavior that day was a major clue that he would soon be leaving Green Bay, as he did for Seattle after the 1998 season. The Holmgren incident got major play in Wisconsin but not nationally. Part of the reason was that Holmgren coached in Green Bay and not New York. Part of the reason was that only a few cameras actually caught the exchange on videotape. Just imagine if Holmgren flipped off and swore at a fan today—how many hits on YouTube would that receive? Holmgren's was the better blowup.

WHAT'S THE BEST TRADE IN PACKERS HISTORY?

32 The NFL is nothing like Major League Baseball. On the diamond, players can adjust to new teams pretty easily, making trades in baseball more frequent and more productive. A trade nowadays in the NFL is rare. Most transactions in football are for low-round draft picks or for players only the Mel Kipers of the world know or care about. But some deals, past and present, have turned into gold. For example, in 2000, Ron Wolf sent underachieving cornerback Fred Vinson and a sixth-round pick to the Seahawks for Ahman Green and a fifth-round pick. Green ran for more yards than any Packer not named Jim Taylor. Great trade.

Lombardi's Packers teams were built largely through the draft. However, a couple of key components came to Green Bay through trades. For example, in 1959, Lombardi sent linebacker Marv Matuzak to the Baltimore Colts for guard Fuzzy Thurston. All Thurston did was help solidify an offensive line that would protect Bart Starr and open holes for Paul Hornung and Jim Taylor. The Packers would go on to win five NFL championships, including the first two Super Bowls.

In 2007, eight days before the season opener, Packers GM Ted Thompson lived up to his name, "Trader Ted," and sent a sixth-round draft pick to the Giants for running back Ryan Grant, who was buried on New York's depth chart. Grant started the final seven games of the season and rushed for 956 yards and 8 touchdowns. His finest moment came in the "Snow Globe" game in the NFC Divisional Playoffs against the Seahawks. After fumbling twice in the opening quarter, Grant stormed back to gain 201 yards and score 3 touchdowns in Green Bay's 42–20 victory.

These were three great trades, but they only get honorable mention. Here are the five best trades in Packers history.

5. JOHN MARTINKOVIC TO THE NEW YORK GIANTS FOR A THIRD-ROUND DRAFT CHOICE, 1958

This deal was one of the few bright spots in Ray "Scooter" McLean's only season leading the Packers, although at the time, it didn't look like such a great deal, since Martinkovic made the Pro Bowl three times during his stay in Green Bay, and all McLean got back was a third-round draft pick. However, McLean made the most of the selection, choosing a fullback out of Illinois named Ray Nitschke. Actually, Nitschke had played a little linebacker for the Fighting

Illini, as well, and by 1960, he had become the man in the middle for a Packers dynasty. Martinkovic was eventually elected to the Packers Hall of Fame, but Nitschke is not only remembered in Green Bay's Hall of Fame, but also the Pro Football Hall of Fame in Canton, Ohio.

4. DON HORN TO THE DENVER BRONCOS FOR ALDEN ROCHE AND A FIRST-ROUND DRAFT PICK, 1971

On paper, the deal doesn't look like much. Don Horn was a fourth-year quarterback best known for backing up Bart Starr. Horn's best season was in 1969, when he led the Packers in passing yards and threw 11 touchdowns to go with 11 interceptions. Horn does own a place in Packers history—he was the first Packers quarterback to throw for more than 400 yards in a game, throwing for 410 yards against the St. Louis Cardinals in a 45–28 win at Lambeau Field in December 1969. But Horn was expendable and was sent packing to Denver. In return, Green Bay received Alden Roche, a 6'4", 255-pound defensive end who was solid and steady. He started for five seasons and won the team's MVP award on defense in 1971. But the jewel in the trade was Denver's first-round draft pick, ninth overall, which the Packers used to select running back John Brockington.

Brockington was the first Packer to rush for more than 1,000 yards in each of his first three seasons with the team. His 5,024 rushing yards ranks third on the Packers' all-time list. Brockington was inducted into the Packers Hall of Fame in 1984. As for Horn? He played 11 games over two uneventful seasons with the Broncos, and then played a year with the Browns and then a year with the Chargers before finishing up his playing career with the Portland Thunder of the old WFL.

3. A FOURTH-ROUND DRAFT PICK TO THE CLEVELAND BROWNS FOR HENRY JORDAN, 1959

As good of a coach as Vince Lombardi was, he was just as shrewd a general manager. In one of his first moves leading the Packers, Lombardi sent a fourth-round draft pick to Cleveland for defensive tackle Henry Jordan. The Browns would take little-known fullback Bob Jarus with the pick, while Jordan became the mainstay in the middle of the Packers' defensive line during their 1960s dynasty.

2. A. D. WILLIAMS TO THE BROWNS FOR WILLIE DAVIS, 1960

The more you read about the Packers dynasty of the 1960s, the more you realize how important trades were to the success of the team. Somehow, some way, just a year after stealing Henry Jordan from Cleveland, Lombardi was able to talk the Browns into trading Willie Davis to Green Bay for offensive lineman A. D. Williams. Davis was a 17th-round draft pick but still played in every game for his first two seasons in Cleveland. Davis then started 138 straight games for the Packers and anchored a defensive line that won five titles for Lombardi.

Davis played before sacks were an official stat. He does, however, own the Packers' franchise record for fumble recoveries (21) and was a five-time All-Pro. Davis was inducted into the Pro Football Hall of Fame in 1981. It's not often you give up next to nothing for a Hall of Famer, but that's what happened when Lombardi traded for Willie Davis

1. A FIRST-ROUND DRAFT PICK TO THE ATLANTA FALCONS FOR BRETT FAVRE, 1992

As rare as trades are in the modern era in the NFL, a block-buster deal is even more unique. At the time of this trade, the word *blockbuster* probably wasn't used, but looking back, it's a trade that changed history for Ron Wolf and the Green Bay Packers. Not even three months on the job, the new GM knew he needed a franchise quarterback and wanted to right a wrong that had stayed with him for almost a year.

Wolf was with the Jets on draft day in 1991, when he tried desperately to move up to take Favre in the second round. It didn't happen, and the Falcons took Favre with the Jets on deck. In the same 1991 draft, the Packers moved down in the first round in a trade with the Eagles. The Packers received the Eagles' first-round pick in 1992 to make that move.

Days after Wolf was hired in Green Bay in November 1991, in the first game he watched as GM, the Packers lost to the Falcons in Atlanta. Before the game, Wolf found out that Favre was available and he scouted the player he so coveted. On February 10, 1992, Wolf made the trade that would define his career. He sent the extra 1992 first-round draft pick the Packers had received from the Eagles the year before to the Falcons for Brett Favre.

Wolf admitted that he had to sell the executive committee on Favre before pulling off the trade. "I told them what I thought," said Wolf. "I said people are going to be in the stands, they're going to be wearing number 4 jerseys. This is what I envision. He's going to be a great quarterback and he's going to turn this whole franchise around and he did that."

Favre made Wolf look like a genius. He turned into a Hall of Fame caliber quarterback. The Falcons, meanwhile, traded down two spots in the first round, using that Packers pick. They eventually selected running back Tony Smith—ironically, from the same college as Favre, Southern Mississippi. Smith started six games in three seasons with the Falcons, rushing for 329 yards and two touchdowns in his career.

WHAT'S THE WORST TRADE IN PACKERS HISTORY?

33 The Packers have had their share of clunkers, too—like giving up Matt Hasselbeck to the Seahawks to move up in the first round in 2001 so they could draft defensive end Jamal Reynolds. Another forgettable deal came back in 1973, when Dan Devine gave up two second-round draft picks, in 1974 and 1975, for quarterback Jim Del Gaizo. Del Gaizo lasted one season in Green Bay, played eight games, started two, completed 43.5 percent of his passes, and threw just two touchdowns to go with six interceptions. Remarkably, these two deals do not even make the Packers wall of shame. Look no farther—here are the three worst trades in Packers history.

3. 1985 MOSSY CADE TRADE

A defensive back from Texas, Cade was drafted with the sixth overall pick in 1984 by the San Diego Chargers. Cade turned his back on the NFL and played instead for the Memphis Showboats in his rookie season. The Chargers wanted nothing more than to find a suitor for

Cade, and they found one in Forrest Gregg and the Green Bay Packers.

Cade became a Packer on September 5, 1985, three days before the opener. The Packers sent the Chargers a first-round draft pick in 1986 and a conditional pick in 1987 (which turned into a fifth-rounder). Cade played two seasons for the Packers and intercepted five passes in his career, but it's what happened off the field that made this trade look so bad. Cade was found guilty of two counts of sexual assaulting a member of his family in May 1987. The crime had occurred in November 1985, during his first season in Green Bay, at his DePere home. Cade was sentenced to 15 months in prison in 1987 and never played another down in the NFL.

2. 1981 JOHN JEFFERSON TRADE

This trade ranks so high because of how much the Packers had to give up in order to get wide receiver John Jefferson. Green Bay sent San Diego a 1982 second-rounder, a 1983 first-rounder, and a 1984 second-rounder, and the teams swapped positions in the first round of the 1982 draft. Plus, the Packers threw in another wideout, Aundra Thompson.

Jefferson came to Green Bay with an impressive resume: three straight 1,000-yard seasons, with double-digit touchdowns each year. Jefferson averaged 66 catches a year in San Diego and made the Pro Bowl in each of his first three seasons. In a Packers uniform, Jefferson averaged just three catches a game in four seasons. His numbers are skewed somewhat due to the players' strike in 1982, but in all, Jefferson caught just 11 touchdowns in his four seasons and never topped the 1,000-yard mark. He finished his career in Green Bay playing 50 games and catching 149 passes for 2,253 yards. Decent numbers, yes, but not good enough to give away a first- and two second-round draft picks.

1. 1974 JOHN HADL TRADE

Until Herschel Walker became the apple of the Vikings' eye, the John Hadl trade was widely considered the worst trade in NFL history. The Packers were 3–3 six games into the 1974 season when Dan Devine decided to pull off a deal that would cripple the Packers for years to come. The Packers sent the Rams first-, second-, and third-round draft picks in 1975 and first- and third-round draft choices in 1976 for a 34-year-old quarterback named John Hadl. If you had to defend the deal, you would say that Hadl had been the reigning NFC Player of the Year when he led the Rams to the NFC West crown in 1973. But this was his 13th season in pro football, and he wasn't getting any younger.

Hadl took over the starting job from Jerry Tagge and finished off the season 6–8. Devine then bolted to Notre Dame, handing over a depleted cupboard to favorite son Bart Starr, who was the Packers head coach and general manager. Think about it. The Packers gave up the 9th, 28th, and 61st overall picks in 1975 for Hadl. That's in addition to the 8th and 39th picks overall in 1976. No wonder the Rams were so good and the Packers so bad in the 1970s. Hadl lasted just one more season in Green Bay—his only full season with the Packers, in which he threw 21 interceptions to go with just six touchdowns as the Packers struggled to a 4–10 record. The silver lining (even if that lining was very slim) is that Hadl would be a part of a trade in 1976 that sent Lynn Dickey to Green Bay from the Houston Oilers.

There's no justifying one of the worst trades in NFL history. But it wasn't the worst. Packers fans can thank their neighbors to the west for that. On October 12, 1989, the Cowboys sent running back Herschel Walker and four draft picks to the Minnesota Vikings for five players, six conditional draft picks, and an additional first-rounder. In all, the deal worked out to be three first-rounders, three second-rounders, a third-round pick, and a sixth-round pick for the Cowboys, which led to the Dallas dynasty of the 1990s. Sure, the Hadl trade was the worst in Packers history, but take solace, Packers fans! It wasn't as bad as the Walker trade was for the Vikings.

DOES LEROY BUTLER BELONG IN THE PRO FOOTBALL HALL OF FAME?

34 It's remarkable to think that Reggie White is the only member of the 1996 Packers defense enshrined in the Pro Football Hall of Fame. LeRoy Butler should be No. 2. For some unknown reason, the Hall of Fame selection committee turns its back on safeties. It's the most-ignored defensive position in Canton. Just seven pure safeties are in the Hall of Fame, and the last to be enshrined was Ken Houston in 1980. Butler should get the call.

Critics will point out that Butler was elected to the Pro Bowl only four times in his 12 seasons and named All-Pro four times during that span. Packers safety Willie Wood, who was enshrined in Canton in 1989, was a six-time All-Pro and an eight-time Pro Bowler. Some would argue that Bobby Dillon was the second-best safety in Packers history after Wood. After all, Dillon holds the franchise record with 52 interceptions in just nine seasons during the 1950s. Butler's all-around game and his ability to blitz and yet ball-hawk give him the edge over Dillon.

When you think about a Hall of Famer, ask yourself this question. Was he dominant in his era? LeRoy Butler was dominant in the 1990s. He made the NFL's All-Decade team, and yet he's one of 11 All-Decade safeties since 1960 not currently in the Hall of Fame. Butler was two interceptions from becoming the first player in NFL history to pick off 40 passes along with at least 20 sacks. He was so good that the Denver Broncos designed their entire game plan around minimizing Butler's impact in Super Bowl XXXII. Credit Denver coach Mike Shanahan, since the plan worked, and the Broncos pulled off the upset.

Butler has longevity—he played 12 seasons, all with the Packers, until a shoulder injury forced him to retire in 2002. Certainly, the injury cost him potentially productive years at the tail-end of his career. On the day of announcing his retirement, Butler said of his Hall of Fame chances, "I made the all-decade team [in the 1990s]. I have a shot since that's such a tough team to make. I have more interceptions and sacks combined than any defensive back and I played in two Super Bowls. I think the checklist goes on and on and I think I have a check in most of them."

Butler also invented the "Lambeau Leap" on a blustery December afternoon, the day after Christmas in 1993, against the Oakland Raiders at Lambeau Field. After Butler forced a fumble, Reggie White scooped up the loose ball and began to run until he got tied up. He turned and pitched the ball to Butler, who ran the final 25 yards into the southeast end zone, where he leaped into the arms of the first row of fans. It was a spontaneous celebration that has become the norm for end-zone celebrations, not only in Green Bay but in stadiums across the country. That type of play exemplified the kind of player Butler was. He was a fun-loving, dominant playmaker of his era and one that belongs in the Pro Football Hall of Fame.

BIGGEST BUST: WHO WAS THE WORST DRAFT PICK IN PACKERS HISTORY?

35 For such a storied franchise that oozes history, the Green Bay Packers have had their share of stinkers in the NFL draft. Barty Smith and Jerry Tagge set the standard, which was followed by guys like John Michels, Ahmad Carroll, Antuan Edwards, Brent Fullwood, Mike McCoy, and Alphonso Carreker. If you are looking for a mid-round pick, how about punter B.J. Sander, who Mike Sherman traded up for to select? All of them underachieved in Green Bay, but they only get a dishonorable mention in this space. Here are the five worst draft picks in Packers history.

5. BRUCE CLARK, 1980, FIRST ROUND, FOURTH OVERALL

Bruce Clark was the fourth player selected in the 1980 draft, but the defensive tackle from Penn State would never play a single down in Green Bay for the Packers. Clark chose to play in Canada instead, signing with the

Toronto Argonauts. Eventually, Clark returned home and played seven seasons for the New Orleans Saints and one for the Kansas City Chiefs. What stings is who the Packers could have selected in 1980—future Hall of Famer Art Monk went 14 picks later to the Washington Redskins.

4. RANDY DUNCAN, 1959, FIRST ROUND, FIRST OVERALL

Quarterback Randy Duncan was the first player selected in the 1959 NFL draft, and, like Bruce Clark, he never played a single down at quarterback for the Green Bay Packers. Duncan followed the money trail to the Great White North and wound up in the Canadian Football League, where he played for the British Columbia Lions. Duncan eventually made it back to the states, joining the Dallas Texans of the AFL for one season, where he threw just one touchdown. But Duncan never played in the NFL after being the top pick in the 1959 draft.

3. RICH CAMPBELL, 1981, FIRST ROUND, SIXTH OVERALL

Rich Campbell had so much promise. On paper, he had all of the measurables of an outstanding quarterback. Standing 6'4" and tipping the scales at 215 pounds, Campbell looked the part. Bart Starr bought into the hype and drafted Campbell with the sixth pick in the 1981 draft. Unfortunately, the Packers quickly realized that Campbell's arm was below average, and he never fulfilled the promise of a top-six pick. Most Packers fans think what might have been had the team used that first-round pick to select Hall of Famer Ronnie Lott instead of Campbell. Lott would get drafted two spots after Campbell. All Lott did was help the San Francisco 49ers win eight division titles and four Super Bowls. Campbell played in just seven games in four seasons with the Packers, throwing for only three touchdowns and nine interceptions, with 386 career yards.

2. JAMAL REYNOLDS, 2001, FIRST ROUND, TENTH OVERALL

When you cover draft day in Green Bay, the Packers media relations staff hands out biographies of each player selected. In 2001, they jumped the gun, passing out information about the Packers' top pick that year, linebacker Dan Morgan. A handful of Morgan's biographies had been dished out when they were quickly recalled. That's how close the Packers were to righting a wrong. Instead of Morgan, Mike Sherman selected Jamal Reynolds, an undersized pass-rushing defensive end from Florida State. What made matters worse was that the Packers traded up to get him. The Packers traded away Matt Hasselbeck and the 17th pick in the 2001 first round to move up seven spots and grab Reynolds.

Ron Wolf was on his way out, and technically, he was still the Packers' general manager, but Sherman had already been named his successor, and this was his pick. The big knock on Reynolds was his size, or lack thereof. It wasn't long before Reynolds was known as "Too Small" Jamal. Reynolds lasted just three seasons in Green Bay, collecting just three sacks in 18 career games.

1. TONY MANDARICH, 1989, FIRST ROUND, SECOND OVERALL

I was a student at Wisconsin, which is loaded with Packers fans, when Tony Mandarich was drafted. I can still see a vision from that time that haunts me two decades later: my Packers-loving fraternity brother, Charlie Hill, in his bathrobe, arms heavenward, proclaiming, "A sandwich is a sandwich, but a Mandarich is a Super Bowl!" That kind of hype often surrounded skilled position players like quarterbacks or running backs coming out of college, but never an offensive tackle—until Tony Mandarich.

Mandarich was called "the Incredible Bulk" on the cover of *Sports Illustrated* in the weeks leading up to the 1989 NFL draft, and the magazine called him "the best offensive lineman prospect ever." He was huge, 6'5" and 315 pounds, and he ran like a tight end. The big offensive tackle looked too good to be true—and indeed, he was. Mandarich had a body built by science. Two decades after his playing career ended, he finally admitted that he had used steroids throughout his collegiate career at Michigan State. He then got hooked on painkillers and alcohol in Green Bay.

For years, Packers fans had to relive the Mandarich mistake twice a season, every year, when Barry Sanders and the Lions played Green Bay. Sanders was taken with the third pick in the 1989 draft—the pick after Mandarich. The only bust mentioned with Sanders's name is the one of him in the Hall of Fame. To make the Mandarich mistake sting more, the Chiefs then drafted future Hall of Fame linebacker Derrick Thomas with the fourth pick, and the Falcons nabbed another future Hall of Famer in Deion Sanders with the fifth overall selection. Mandarich lasted three seasons in Green Bay followed by four years out of football and then another three seasons in Indianapolis. He never came close to living up to the hype. Terrified of failing NFL drug tests, Mandarich lost strength and was never the same player he was at Michigan State. If you Google the words "Tony Mandarich bust," you get 118,000 results. That says it all.

THE GREAT FAVRE DEBATE: WHO'S RIGHT AND WHO'S WRONG—BRETT OR TED?

36 Never before in Packers history has there been an episode which divided its fan base like the Brett Favre soap opera of the summer of 2008. The then-retired quarterback wanted to come back, the franchise said it had moved on, and when the dust settled, Favre and the Packers had endured an ugly public divorce resulting in General Manager Ted Thompson trading the legendary quarterback to the New York Jets.

The Brett Favre supporters could not understand why the organization turned its back on football's all-time touchdown leader. There were fan rallies to bring back Favre, as well as websites and T-shirts devoted to the Packers' greatest player of all time. The Ted Thompson/Packers supporters couldn't see why Favre did not understand the word *retired.* Didn't he see that the team had moved on to fourth-year quarterback Aaron Rodgers? Both had strong arguments, but who was right?

Favre says his big mistake was retiring in the first place, claiming the organization pressured him into making a hasty decision. The quarterback claimed the organization failed in keeping lines of communication open between the two parties until it was too late. Favre used his family and agent, James "Bus" Cook, to get his message out early on in the comeback process. Later, Favre simply stated his case to his reporter friends.

The Packers said there was no turning back. Favre had waffled before, and the Packers wanted to move on since he did retire. Not even a month after making his tearful exit from Lambeau Field, Favre was having cold feet and told the organization so, but later, he went back to telling the Packers he was retired for good. The Packers, meanwhile, went ahead and drafted not one, but two quarterbacks the following month and held minicamp practices with Aaron Rodgers as their starting quarterback.

It wasn't until late June that we learned Favre again had the itch to play football. The rumors turned into reports, which turned into quotes from Favre's family members. It was a "weather-balloon" approach, floating quotes to various news outlets to gauge public reaction. Favre was very cognizant of not talking to anyone directly so he could always leave himself an "out" if he chose. But the Packers did not want Favre back, since they had moved on, but they also did not want him playing for another team—especially division-rival Minnesota. The two sides were at a stalemate until training camp began in late July and things got ugly. The big step in the process was Favre filing his reinstatement papers, which negated his retirement. That put the pressure on the Packers. NFL commissioner Roger Goodell took his time approving the reinstatement, giving the organization a chance to figure it all out. But when hours turned to days, Favre was eventually reinstated and wound up flying to Green Bay. This was the turning point. Favre had a face-to-face meeting with Mike McCarthy, during which the Packers' head coach determined that Favre was not committed to playing football for his team in 2008. It was then that Ted Thompson went from being the Packers' general manager to the Packers' general manager who traded Brett Favre. He dealt Favre to the New York Jets for a conditional draft pick, which turned out to be a third-round selection.

There was plenty of blame to go around. Both parties were guilty of poor communication. Favre used his agent and family to get his message out. The Packers tried their best to "take the high road," choosing not to respond to Favre's statements to selected news outlets. However, every so often, information was leaked to the media from their front office. Both sides looked bad. Favre came off as a prima donna—something that went against everything he stood for on the field. He was the ultimate team guy, and yet, through the whole soap opera, Favre put his team in a bad spot.

Nevertheless, the Packers could have easily taken him back, as well. Fans would have forgiven Thompson and McCarthy for going back on their original statements about moving on. This is Brett Favre we are talking about. Before the situation exploded, Cowboys quarterback and Burlington, Wisconsin, native Tony Romo said he understood both sides but knew the value of a guy like Favre, "There are only a handful of guys in the NFL who would be considered top five quarterbacks, and Brett is considered one of those guys. They just don't come around that often." Basically, Romo was saying there are rules and there are exceptions, and Brett Favre would be an exception.

Much was made of the multimillion-dollar, personal-services contract Favre had considered, as these arrangements are commonplace with future hall of fame players. However, the idea was originally broached after Favre retired in March, not when Packers president Mark Murphy visited Favre in Mississippi around the start of training camp. It appeared as if the Packers were "buying" Favre to stay retired. Once again, it was poor communication. McCarthy said, "The train has left the station," but never really communicated to the public why exactly that train had left the station. Was McCarthy worried about losing Aaron Rodgers if Favre was welcomed back? McCarthy never gave a straight-up answer to the question: Which quarterback gave the Packers a better chance to win in 2008, Favre or Rodgers?

The end result was a trade that fans never dreamed of, with Brett Favre wearing a different shade of green and playing for the New York Jets. The summer of 2008 was not the Packers' finest hour, but it wasn't Favre's, either. Who was right? Nobody was right in this situation. Everyone has the right to change his or her mind, but Favre was to blame for the way he came back. The Packers were wrong for letting the situation spiral out of control. It goes back to communication, which neither side did much of.

The Packers will survive, and Brett Favre's legacy will survive—how could it not? After the trade was finalized, Mike McCarthy fittingly said the team would do an "autopsy" of the way the Favre situation was handled by the organization so everyone could learn from the experience. Time heals all wounds, but the point is that it did not have to end that way, and both sides are to blame.

THE BREWERS
AND BRAVES

Milwaukee has a rich baseball tradition. The city's first professional baseball team was the Brewers, who played just one season in 1901 before moving to St. Louis to become the Browns. The Braves came to Milwaukee in 1953 and started an unprecedented love affair with the city, becoming the first big-league club to draw 2 million fans in a season in 1954. Three years later, the Braves won Wisconsin's one and only World Series title. However, the days of drawing 2 million fans were short-lived, and the Braves moved to Atlanta after the 1965 season. Big-league baseball returned to the cream city in 1970, when the Seattle Pilots were sold for $10.5 million to a group led by Allan H. "Bud" Selig and Edmund Fitzgerald, who renamed them the Brewers.

Even though it was once dubbed "Bushville" by the New York Yankees during the 1957 World Series, won by the Braves, Milwaukee has proven over the years that it is one of the great baseball cities in America. The Braves were an instant fan favorite at County Stadium back in the 1950s, while the Brewers set new team records, topping 3 million fans for the first time at Miller Park in 2008.

When searching for the best of the best in Milwaukee baseball, we will consider both the Brewers and the Braves. In many cases, it's a discussion of which player was better on the 1957 Braves versus the 1982 Brewers— arguably the two best teams in Milwaukee baseball. Here are Milwaukee's best on the diamond.

119

WHO MAKES MILWAUKEE'S ALL-TIME TEAM IN BASEBALL?

37 MANAGER

Who's going to manage this collection of All-Stars and clutch players? Fred Haney is a likely choice. He's the man who guided the Milwaukee Braves to back-to-back National League pennants in 1957 and 1958. It would have been three straight, had the Braves won one more game in 1959. Instead, the Braves lost a playoff to the Dodgers and Haney was shown the door. In his three-plus seasons in Milwaukee, Haney won 341 games and lost 231, for a winning percentage of .596—very respectable numbers, but Haney never seemed to win over the Milwaukee fan base. There were calls for his job as early as midyear in 1958, the year after the Braves won the World Series. Even back then, it was, "What have you done for me lately?"

Although Haney has the credentials, the manager choice here is Harvey Kuenn. He's the man who led the 1982 Brewers to their one and only American League pennant.

Kuenn took over for Buck Rodgers 47 games into the season. The Brew Crew's record at the time was 23–24. Under Kuenn, the Brewers won 72 of their final 115 games—the best record in baseball during that span—winning 63 percent of their games en route to the AL East crown.

Like Haney, Kuenn was fired shortly after his team took the city to new heights. Kuenn lasted just one more season; a disappointing fifth-place finish in 1983 ended his run. However, Kuenn proved he was a guy who could manage personalities and talent. He let the Brewers be the Brewers, a fun-loving, hard-nosed group of guys who enjoyed every moment on and off the field. With the hiring of Harvey Kuenn, the pressure was off a team with huge preseason expectations. The players responded by winning 20 of their first 27 games under Kuenn and moved to first place in less than six weeks. The club became known as "Harvey's Wallbangers," a nickname that could not be more perfect.

Kuenn battled health issues. He had stomach and heart surgeries in the 1970s and had his right leg amputated in 1980 after a blood clot gave him circulation issues. Yet, Kuenn's toughness rubbed off on his Brewers. Players respected him and his work ethic and played hard for him. The ideal manager is someone who gets the most out of his club and allows his players to perform at their highest level. For at least one season in 1982, Harvey Kuenn was that man.

38 FIRST BASE

If you were filling out the lineup card for the all-time Milwaukee baseball team, who would start at first base? Do you go with offensive consistency and clutch play in Cecil Cooper, or do you start the young slugger with a high ceiling in Prince Fielder? This is a tough call, and, depending on your perspective, could go either way. Are you arguing for the past, in Cooper, or debating the future, in Fielder? When it's all said and done, we may well be talking about Fielder as the best first baseman in Milwaukee history. However, without psychic insight, Cooper is the choice for the here and now.

You almost can hear it loud and clear: *"Cooooooooop!"* A fan favorite the moment he arrived from the Red Sox in a trade that sent George Scott to Boston, Cecil Cooper wasn't your prototypical first baseman of the late 1970s and 1980s. He wasn't a big bopper. Unlike Fielder, Cooper never hit 50 home runs in a season. In fact, his career high was 32 in 1982, and he finished his career with 241 home runs. But while Cooper didn't hit many out of the park, he hit for average and drove in runs.

Cooper hit .300 or better in his first seven seasons in Milwaukee. He hit a career high .352 in 1980, but he was overshadowed by the AL batting champion that year, George Brett of the Kansas City Royals, who flirted with .400 before finishing the season at .390. Cooper led the American League in runs batted in twice, in 1980 and 1983, and still holds the Brewers' record, with 126 RBI in 1983. Cooper was a five-time All-Star and a three-time winner of the Silver Slugger Award (1980–1982).

Prince Fielder can swing the bat. Graced with a powerful left-handed swing, in 2007, Fielder was the youngest player in baseball history to belt 50 home runs in a season, breaking the record held by Willie Mays. The 50 home runs not only set a new franchise mark, but also set a Milwaukee baseball record, breaking Eddie Mathews's 47 in 1953. It's still too early to determine the ceiling on Fielder, but there's no question that the kid can hit.

There are two major factors that separate Cooper from Fielder. Cooper won two Gold Glove Awards (1979–1980), something that Fielder will never do because of his average fielding abilities. Plus, Cooper was one of the ultimate clutch hitters. While Fielder hit a big walk-off home run in the final week of the 2008 season, the big guy had a rough postseason debut, going 1 for 14 (.071) in the Brewers' divisional series against the Phillies. Cooper, meanwhile, led the Brewers out of a 2–0 deficit against the California Angles in the American League Championship Series. Cooper's seventh-inning single in Game 5 drove in the tying and winning runs, sending the Brewers to their one and only World Series. In Milwaukee, most Brewers fans view Cooper begging the ball to "get down" against the Angels as Red Sox Nation pictures Carlton Fisk "waving" his home run fair in the 1975 World Series.

It seems likely that Fielder may one day surpass the achievements of Cecil Cooper. For now, "Coop" is the man.

39 SECOND BASE

The two greatest teams in Milwaukee baseball history were the 1957 Braves and the 1982 Brewers so, many of the debates center around the major players of those two clubs. That's certainly the case at second base with Jim Gantner and Red Schoendienst. If this was simply a comparison of 1982 Gantner versus 1957 Schoendienst, Red would win a close argument based strictly on numbers. Schoendienst played a pivotal role in helping Milwaukee to its one and only World Series title. Many credit the acquisition of Schoendienst as adding the missing piece to the puzzle for the Braves. After getting traded to Milwaukee from the New York Giants, the redhead hit .310 in 93 games and played terrific defense, helping the Braves to the National League pennant. By comparison, Gantner hit .295 in 1982 with four home runs, 43 RBI, and six stolen bases, helping the Brewers to their one and only American League pennant. However, who was the better player in their respective careers while playing in Milwaukee? Schoendienst is a Hall of Famer, but based on Milwaukee playing time, the nod goes to the guy they called "Gumby."

If you Google Gantner's name, the word *unheralded* is associated with his biography on multiple websites. His career numbers may not astound you. He was a career .274 hitter with 1,696 hits and 47 home runs. However, Gantner's value boils down to more than statistics. He played his whole 17-season career in Milwaukee—something few baseball players can say these days. He was a fun-loving, scrappy, hard-working, homegrown talent from Fond du Lac who played college ball at UW–Oshkosh. His storybook career with the Brewers began in 1976—he appeared in his first game as a pinch runner for Hank Aaron, who had reached base in the final at-bat of his career. Gantner was a "glue guy," someone who would organize pregame competitions just for fun. Many remember Jim Gantner as the soul of the 1982 Brewers.

Schoendienst spent just four of his 19 big-league seasons in Milwaukee, and his numbers while playing in the Beer City were rather pedestrian. He did collect 200 hits in 1957, but almost half of those hits came in the Big Apple as a member of the Giants, prior to his trade to Milwaukee. In his four seasons as a Brave, Schoendienst hit .278 with eight home runs and 75 RBI. He was tough. He played 109 games in 1958 despite a broken finger, bruised ribs, and pleurisy when the Braves won their second straight NL pennant. He also lost nearly all of 1959 with tuberculosis and was eventually traded to St. Louis after the 1960 season. There's no question that Schoendienst was a key cog in the Braves machine that appeared in back-to-back

World Series. But Gantner represents the best second baseman in Milwaukee history.

Gantner is forever linked with two Hall of Famers from that 1982 team: Robin Yount and Paul Molitor. But Gumby's a Hall of Famer himself, albeit not in Cooperstown. Rather, his plaque sits on Fourth Street in the Wisconsin Sports Hall of Fame. Gantner is so highly regarded in the state that there's an ongoing debate about whether the Brewers should retire his number 17. That's a question for the Brewers brass to answer. However, there's no question that Jim Gantner is the best second baseman in Wisconsin baseball history.

THIRD BASE

How impressive was the left-handed swing of Eddie Mathews? Ty Cobb once called it perfect, one of three or four perfect swings "the Georgia Peach" ever laid eyes on. The sweet swing of Mathews can be found on the cover of the very first issue of *Sports Illustrated* in 1954. Mathews was a big, left-handed third baseman who socked 512 home runs in his career. His 486 home runs as a third baseman stood for almost 20 years before Mike Schmidt broke his record.

Mathews is the only player to have played for the Braves in Boston, Milwaukee, and Atlanta. He played his rookie year in obscurity in Boston, only to blossom in Milwaukee. Mathews went from hitting .242 with 25 home runs and

58 RBI in Beantown in 1952 to slugging 47 home runs and knocking in 135 RBI while hitting .302 in front of huge crowds during his first season in the Beer City. Mathews would lead the league in home runs twice and be named to nine All-Star teams. He was the perfect complement to right-handed slugger Hank Aaron.

Milwaukee has had its share of quality third baseman—All-Stars like Tommy Harper (1970), Don Money (four times, twice at third base in 1974 and 1976), and Paul Molitor (two of his five All-Star appearances were at the hot corner). The Brewers also sent third basemen Kevin Seitzer (1995) and Jeff Cirillo (1997) to the Midsummer Classic. Molitor makes the best argument against Mathews, but he played just 29 percent of his 2,683 career games at third base. Don Money deserves consideration, ranking sixth on the Brewers' all-time hits list with 1,168. He also hit 134 home runs during his 11 seasons in Milwaukee. Money's biggest home-run year was 1977, when he belted out 25 long balls. Mathews hit 25 or more home runs 12 times with the Braves. End of argument.

Mathews stands above them all. The modern-day baseball fan might miss just how great of a player Mathews was. He played 2,181 games at third base—seventh on baseball's all-time list. Those 512 home runs put him in the top 10 at the time of his retirement in 1968. Maybe we don't appreciate Mathews more since he fell short of 3,000 hits (2,315). Or maybe it's because he struggled in the postseason (.227 in the 1957 World Series and .160 with 11 strikeouts in the 1958 World Series). Whatever the reason, Eddie Mathews is one of the more underrated players in baseball history. He was elected to the Baseball Hall of Fame in 1978 in his fifth attempt. However, there's no second-guessing that he's the greatest third baseman in Milwaukee history and one of the best of all time.

SHORTSTOP

Robin Yount played more games at short-stop (1,479) than in the outfield (1,218), so we will put "the Kid" at short. You might think this a no-brainer, slam dunk for Yount but let's not discount J.J. Hardy. Granted, Hardy is now entering the prime of his big-league career, but his numbers rate favorably against the Hall of Famer.

In his first four seasons, Hardy hit .270 with 64 home runs and 218 RBI and was voted to the NL All-Star team in his third season. Yount hit .266 with 17 home runs and 181 RBI and had yet to be invited to the Midsummer Classic. Also consider that Hardy played 113 fewer games than Yount during his first four years after missing most of his sophomore season with an ankle injury. Yount did steal 51 bases to Hardy's five. However, the biggest discrepancy between the two young shortstops is defense. Yount committed 120 errors in his first four years, Hardy just 40. Hardy may have the early edge on Yount, but there's no way of knowing how his promising career will end. Yount is a proven Hall of Famer and gets the nod on his complete body of work.

Yount began his big-league career as an 18-year-old rookie in Milwaukee back in 1974. Some young players can't handle life in "the show," but Yount showed some incredible talent and never left Milwaukee. He was the youngest player in the American League for two straight seasons (1974–1975), and in 1976, he was the youngest player ever to play in at least 161 games. "I was here when Robin Yount first broke into the league," Hank Aaron once said. "I saw greatness in him even then." There were growing pains defensively at shortstop for Yount, but by 1982, he had won a Gold Glove Award. Yount was open to new challenges, and he moved to center field in 1985 to lessen the wear and tear on his body. He became a solid outfielder almost instantly. Who could forget his diving catch in 1987, preserving Juan Nieves's no-hitter? It's still the only no-no in franchise history.

Why is Yount so special? "Consistency and the ability to produce in the clutch," says WISN sports director Dan Needles, who covered Yount during the last half of his playing career. Yount came up big when the stakes were the highest. The Brewers clinched the American League East on the final day of the 1982 season, thanks to two huge home runs by Yount off another future Hall of

129

Famer, Jim Palmer. Yount batted .414 in his one and only World Series.

Former Brewers owner Bud Selig used to get razzed for his fondness of Yount. Opposing players and front-office personnel would often tease Selig by calling Yount his kid—as in, "Bud, *your* kid did this." Selig would laugh it off, because in a sense, it was true. He once said of Yount, "If I ever had a son, he'd be the son I'd like to have." Selig is a big reason why Yount spent all of his 20 seasons in Milwaukee. Selig convinced Yount to stay put rather than test free agency back in 1989.

Yount played shortstop in his first 11 seasons and in the outfield for the rest of his career. He won two MVP Awards—one at each of those two different positions. Yount collected more hits (1,731) in the 1980s than any other player in baseball. Even though he won his second MVP in 1989, his best season was 1982. Yount had career highs in home runs (29), runs batted in (114), and batting average (.331). Most importantly, Yount led the Brewers to their first and only World Series appearance.

If Jim Gantner was the soul of that 1982 club, Yount was the heart. He hit .414 in the 1982 World Series, leading the Brewers in their classic seven-game series against the St. Louis Cardinals.

Yount collected career hit number 3,000 on September 9, 1992, during a 5–4 loss to the Cleveland Indians. Many Brewers fans still recall play-by-play man Bob Uecker's call,

"Three thousand...for Robin!" On that day, Yount joined Willie Mays as the only big leaguers with at least 3,000 hits, 200 home runs, 200 stolen bases, and 100 triples.

Yount was the symbol of the Brewers franchise for three separate decades. He was the consummate team player. Former teammate and fellow Hall of Famer Paul Molitor said, "For me in some ways to be an unselfish player was work. For him it was a lot more natural."

Yount's number 19 is one of four numbers retired by the Milwaukee Brewers. He was elected into the Baseball Hall of Fame in 1999.In his induction speech, he said, "The game of life can sometimes be too short, so play it with everything you got."

42 RIGHT FIELD

You can make the argument that Hank Aaron was the greatest outfielder in baseball history, not just in Milwaukee. His numbers are astounding. Those who know him best say he's a better human being than a baseball player, and that is really saying something. To generations of baseball fans, he's baseball's home-run king, no matter what the record book says. Hank Aaron is a perfect example of what an ambassador for baseball should be.

On the field, Aaron's best season was 1957, when he was the National League's Most Valuable Player. He socked 44 home runs that season and knocked in a career-high 132 runs. Most importantly, that year, he led Milwaukee to the city's one and only World Series title.

Aaron played his first 12 seasons in Milwaukee before moving with the Braves to Atlanta. He was an 11-time All-Star while playing in Milwaukee. In his career, he was selected to play in the Midsummer Classic a remarkable 21 times. Aaron was the model of consistency, hitting 20 or more home runs in 20 straight seasons. Aside from his rookie year, "Hammerin' Hank" hit at least 24 home runs and knocked in at least 92 runs a season and hit a minimum average of .292.

It's tough to even come up with names to enter into a conversation about Aaron. Rob Deer? Charlie Moore? Jeromy Burnitz? Sixto Lezcano? All four players were mainstays for the Brewers in right field at one point or another. The four sluggers *combined* for 693 home runs in their big-league careers. Aaron finished his career with 755 home runs.

Aaron hit 470 of those 755 home runs (62 percent) during the 14 seasons he called Milwaukee home. (Aaron played his final two seasons for the Brewers in 1975 and 1976). Aaron was inducted into the Baseball Hall of Fame in 1982 and is one of four Brewers to have his number retired. Aaron's number 44 is also retired by the Atlanta Braves. Hank Aaron is the greatest player in Milwaukee baseball history and one of the best players in the history of Major League Baseball.

43 CENTER FIELD

Granted, Ben Ogilvie predominantly played left field alongside Gorman Thomas in the Brewers' outfield, but since neither would beat out Ryan Braun in left field or Hank Aaron in right, let's have some fun and compare the two head to head. Many Brewers fans might take "Stormin'" Gorman Thomas over Ben Ogilvie and they could make a case. Thomas was an acrobatic center fielder for Harvey's Wallbangers in 1982 and the first Brewers playoff club in 1981. He was a hard-nosed slugger who hit home runs but struck out a lot. He was a fan favorite for his fearless play. Thomas just looked the part of a Milwaukee hero, with his long hair springing out from his ball cap and his trademark early-1980s bushy mustache.

Ben Ogilvie, on the other hand, was just the opposite in appearance. The Panamanian was known for his huge forearms and strong wrists. He was a bit more introverted, making him less of a crowd-pleaser, but on the field, he was a fierce competitor whose numbers might surprise you.

Ogilvie played nine of his 16 major-league seasons in Milwaukee. He discovered his power stroke with the Brewers and led the league with 41 home runs in 1980. Ogilvie was a three-time All-Star and finished his career with 235 home runs—176 of those in a Brewers uniform. He hit three home runs in a game on three separate occasions. Despite his skill with the bat, Ogilvie might be best known for what he did with his glove on the final day of

133

the 1982 regular season. The Brewers and Orioles were tied and played a winner-take-all finale in Baltimore. With the game in doubt, Ogilvie made a sliding catch in the left-field corner that preserved the game and the division title for the Brewers.

Thomas grabbed more headlines with his titanic blasts. He made just one All-Star team (1980) but was a force in the 6-hole for those Brewers playoff teams. Thomas had a good eye at the plate (98 walks in 1979), but also struck out a ton (175 strikeouts in 1979, 143 in 1982). He was a slugger who could field—a rarity in baseball. Thomas finished his career with 268 home runs—208 with the Brewers. He led the league twice in home runs (45 in 1979 and 39 in 1982). Thomas played in Milwaukee for all but two of his big-league seasons but finished his Milwaukee years hitting just .230.

What's the verdict? This one is a tough call, but take Ogilvie for his consistency. He hit .280 or better in six of his nine seasons in Milwaukee, and he could hit the long ball, as well. Thomas had too many strikeouts. Ogilvie put the ball in play more than Thomas, so it's no wonder he hit fifth and Thomas hit sixth in the batting order during their peak seasons. Ogilvie gets the nod, and we'll rely on his athleticism to handle center field.

LEFT FIELD

His playing career is still in its infancy, but Ryan Braun has already proven he's one of the best ever to play baseball in Milwaukee. Braun won the 2007 NL Rookie of the Year Award, even though he spent the first seven weeks of the season in the minors. He was the Brewers' first-round draft pick in 2005 and immediately lived up to the hype. In one of the greatest rookie seasons in baseball history, Braun hit .324 with 34 home runs, 97 RBI, and 15 stolen bases in just 113 games. After his first two seasons, Braun owned 71 home runs, which ties Albert Pujols for fourth-most in Major League Baseball history, behind Joe DiMaggio, Ralph Kiner, and former Milwaukee Brave Eddie Mathews. He reached 50 home runs in his career faster than anyone in big-league history other than Mark McGwire. In 2008, Braun became the first Brewers outfielder to be voted to start an All-Star Game.

When you look at the Brewers' record book, the name Geoff Jenkins appears all over the place. He ranks in the top five in hits, extra-base hits, total bases, runs, doubles, RBI, and games played. Jenkins ranks second in home runs (212) in Brewers history, behind Robin Yount. He was a solid outfielder, spending most of his Milwaukee career in left field. Jenkins spent 10 seasons in Milwaukee and always seemed to be on the cusp of superstardom, but for one reason or another, it never happened. He did make the NL All-Star team in 2003. The one thing he failed to do was drive in more than 100 runs, though he came close, with 90 or more RBI on three separate occasions. Jenkins was a terrific clubhouse guy, tremendous with the media, and he was a solid outfielder with the Brewers for a decade, but we'll give the nod to the young up-and-comer, Ryan Braun.

Admittedly, Braun struggled defensively his rookie year, when he committed 26 errors at third base, but he did manage to make a smooth transition to left field before his sophomore season. In fact, Braun did not commit a single error in 148 starts in 2008 and recorded nine outfield assists.

Braun also excels in the clutch. When the Brewers needed him most, Braun stepped up. Playing through a painful oblique strain, Braun slugged a walk-off, grand-slam home run during the final week of the 2008 season to win a crucial game against the Pirates. And he saved his best for last—in the regular-season finale against the Cubs, with the game tied 1–1, Braun hit a two-run, eighth-inning home run to give the Brewers the winning margin. The victory, coupled with the Mets losing to the Marlins in the final game played at Shea Stadium, meant that the Brewers ended a 26-year playoff drought as they won the National League wild card.

Braun is also a streaky hitter. His home runs come in bunches. His eight home runs in eight games in May 2008 was a first in Brewers franchise history. During that run,

Braun signed an eight-year contract worth $45 million. At the time, it was the largest contract in big-league history for a player not eligible for arbitration. "It's a big moment in Brewers history," Brewers general manger Doug Melvin said. Braun followed up with, "It's unprecedented. That means a lot to me." It's historic money based on one of the greatest first years in baseball history. Braun hasn't disappointed yet, and the Brewers hope he will be worth every penny.

CATCHER

This is perhaps the most even debate of all of the baseball arguments. Depending on who you ask, you could make a case for either Ted Simmons or Del Crandall as the best catcher. It's win-win taking either player, but this argument's for Ted Simmons.

Del Crandall played 11 of his 16 seasons in Milwaukee. He was an eight-time All-Star and a four-time Gold Glove winner. Ted Simmons was an eight-time All-Star, as well, although just two of his eight trips were as a Brewer. Simmons played just five of his 21 seasons in Milwaukee. Crandall finished his Milwaukee career with an average of .259 (1953–1963), while Simmons hit .262 during his time in the Beer City (1981–1985). Crandall averaged 14.7 home runs and 49 RBI a year in Milwaukee. Simmons averaged 13.2 home runs but 79 RBI while playing for the Brewers.

Crandall's a member of the Braves Hall of Fame, and his calling card was his defense. There's no question that he was a better defensive backstop than Simmons, who was considered an average defensive catcher at best. However, the offense Simmons provided for his team outweighs the defensive contributions Crandall gave his club. Crandall's best offensive season was in 1958, when he hit .272, drove in 63 runs, and knocked out 18 homers. Crandall's numbers during the World Series–winning season of 1957: .253 average, 15 home runs, and 46 RBI. Simmons's two best seasons came in the pennant-winning year of 1982 and in 1983, when he averaged 18 home runs and 103 RBI. Crandall's average bat is the reason why Simmons wins this argument by a sliver.

46 DESIGNATED HITTER

There is no question that Paul Molitor belongs on our collective best Milwaukee baseball team. The big question surrounding Molitor is where to play him. Molitor started his career as a second baseman who played some shortstop. He dabbled in the outfield and then manned the hot corner for a few seasons. Molitor spent his last eight seasons primarily as a designated hitter. In his 21-year career, Molitor played 1,174 games at DH, 791 at third base, 400 at second base, 197 at first base, 57 at shortstop, and 50 in the outfield. At the 2008 All-Star Game at the old Yankee Stadium, Major League Baseball recognized past living Hall of Famers and had them run out to their places on the field. Molitor was the lone DH. Since he was a DH for 44 percent of the games he played in, Molitor will be a DH for our Milwaukee's best.

Since the American League approved the designated-hitter rule in 1973, the Braves are out of this conversation, as are the current Brewers after their switch to the National League in 1998. There were a couple of other Brewers, though, who deserve a mention. George Scott played five seasons in Milwaukee and was a fan favorite. "The Boomer" is one of five Brewers to lead their league in home runs, as he did in 1975, with 36. Scott also led the AL that season with 109 RBI. He was a big man and yet had great hands and was incredibly athletic. He won five Gold Gloves at first base and only served as a DH 21 times in his final three seasons in Milwaukee.

The other designated hitter who gets an honorable mention is Dave Parker. "The Cobra" spent just the 1990 season in Milwaukee but hit well enough to be named to the American League squad in the Midsummer Classic. Parker hit 21 home runs with 92 RBI while hitting .289 in his one and only season with the Brewers. Both Parker and Scott were good, solid hitters but must step aside next to Paul Molitor.

The man known as "the Ignitor" burst onto the Milwaukee scene in 1978, when he finished second in the voting for American League Rookie of the Year. Like fellow Hall of

Famer Robin Yount, Molitor spent just 64 games in the minors before coming up to the big leagues for good. Molitor made five All-Star teams in his 15 seasons in Milwaukee. Of his 3,319 career hits, Molitor produced 2,281 of those in a Brewers uniform—second to Yount on the club's all-time list. He was the first to collect five hits in one game in the World Series. His 412 stolen bases remain a Brewers record.

The big knock on Molitor was his inability to stay healthy. He missed more than 500 games in his career due to injury. That's more than three seasons lost. Think about how many *more* hits he'd have had if he wasn't hurt so often early in his career. How important was Molitor to the lineup? In 1987, the Brewers went 76–41 when Molitor played, but 22–23 in games he missed.

The 1987 Brewers team was known at "Team Streak." The club started the season 13–0, and then a month later lost 12 straight. Individually, Molitor put together one of the greatest streaks of all, hitting safely in 39 straight games in the summer of 1987. It's the fifth-longest hitting streak after 1900, and the second-longest (to Pete Rose's 44) since Joe DiMaggio's record of 56 straight in 1941. The streak was finally broken on Wednesday, August 26, against the Indians. Rick Manning may be the only player in baseball history to get booed for winning a game after he drove in the winning run for the Brewers with Molitor and the streak left hanging in the on-deck circle.

Molitor was and still is one of the most popular Brewers of all time. Even though he left Milwaukee to sign a four-year free-agent contract worth $13 million with the Toronto Blue Jays in 1993, he received a standing ovation when he returned to County Stadium. He would go on to win a World Series with the Blue Jays in 1993, but he went into the Baseball Hall of Fame in 2004 following Robin Yount as the second member to wear a Brewers cap on his plaque. His number 4 has been retired by the Brewers, and he is one of the best pure hitters in Milwaukee history.

47 RIGHT-HANDED STARTING PITCHER

Brewers fans think of Pete Vuckovich for this one, no-brainer. After all, Vuke won the American League Cy Young Award during the Brew Crew's pennant-winning season of 1982. There's no question, the big right-hander was gifted and dominant. He went 32–10 during 1981 and 1982. However, Vuke won just eight games for the Brewers in the four following seasons. If you take a look at the numbers, they lean toward Lew Burdette as the greatest right-handed pitcher in Milwaukee history.

Burdette was the model of consistency. From 1953 to 1961, he won at least 13 games a season for the Milwaukee Braves. That included back-to-back 20-win seasons in 1958 and 1959.

The pinnacle of Burdette's career came in the 1957 World Series. He dominated the mighty Yankees, won three of the four games for the Braves and earned the Most Valuable Player Award with an ERA of 0.67. All three wins were complete games, including a victory in Game 7 at Yankee Stadium that clinched the one and only World Series title in Milwaukee history. Burdette was magnificent in the series, throwing 24 straight scoreless innings, which included two shutouts. Burdette beat three different Yankees starters in the series: Bobby Shantz in Game 2, Hall of Famer Whitey Ford in Game 5, and Don Larsen in Game 7.

Burdette won 203 games in his career—173 of those in Milwaukee. Vuckovich won 93 games, which included 40 victories over five years in Milwaukee. Yes, Vuckovich has a Cy Young Award that no one can take away, but Lew Burdette wins the title of best right-handed pitcher in Milwaukee baseball.

48 LEFT-HANDED STARTING PITCHER

Can you imagine a big-league hitter being fearful of a little 42-year-old pitcher? That was the story back in 1963, when Warren Spahn went a remarkable 23–7. Imagine—23–7! And the 42-year-old Spahn managed to throw 22 complete games that year. Think about that for a minute. A 42-year-old who was maybe 6 feet tall and 175 pounds dripping wet finished 22 of the 33 games he started that season. To put it into perspective, C. C. Sabathia had 10 complete games during his incredible 2008 season.

Sabathia was traded from the Indians to the Brewers on July 7, 2008, and turned in the greatest second half in Milwaukee baseball history at any position. The 6'7" Sabathia overpowered hitters, winning 11 of his 17 starts in Milwaukee and striking out almost one batter per inning pitched. What made his run even more impressive? He pitched his final three starts on three days rest to help the Brewers snap their 26-year playoff drought. It was fitting that Sabathia was on the hill when the Brewers clinched their wild-card win against the Cubs on the final day of the regular season in 2008.

Although he produced one of the greatest stretches of pitching in modern baseball history, Sabathia's stay in Milwaukee lasted four months. After the season, he signed the richest free-agent contract ever by a pitcher when he went to play for the New York Yankees, thanks to a seven-year deal worth $161 million. Much was made about Sabathia pitching on short rest, especially with free agency on the horizon, but for Warren Spahn, that's just the way the game was played back in his day.

Spahn pitched for the Milwaukee Braves in the prime of his career, from 1953 to 1964. In those 12 seasons, he won more than 60 percent of his games, going 234–154. He won 20 or more games 13 times in his career ,which included a streak of six straight 20-win seasons. He led the Braves to back-to-back National League pennants in 1957 and 1958, winning 43 games in those two seasons. He won the Cy Young Award in 1957. Spahn was a decent stick, too, hitting 35 home runs during his 21-year career.

Now imagine what numbers Spahn could have racked up had he not missed three seasons at the start of his career to serve his country in World War II. Spahn was a combat engineer who fought in the Battle of the Bulge and earned both the Purple Heart and the Bronze Star. Spahn said his war experience gave his baseball career perspective; he never took the game too seriously.

Warren Spahn isn't just the best left-handed pitcher in Milwaukee baseball history; he's the greatest lefty to play anywhere. Of the 13 seasons in his career that he won 20 games, nine of those were in Milwaukee. His 363 career victories are the most in baseball history by a southpaw, and he ranks fifth on baseball's all-time wins list. Spahn was elected to the Baseball Hall of Fame in 1973 on the first ballot.

49 RELIEF PITCHER

On the surface, the question almost seems almost laughable. Who's the best closer in Milwaukee history, Hall of Famer Rollie Fingers or journeyman Dan Plesac? But when you take a closer look at it, you could make a case for either one being the best closer in Milwaukee baseball history.

Plesac is no pushover. The left-hander was a three-time All-Star for the Brewers in the late 1980s and early 1990s. Plesac saved 165 games during his seven seasons in Milwaukee. He saved 30 games in 1986 and 33 games for "Team Streak" back in 1987. But let's be honest—as good as Dan Plesac was, he was no Rollie Fingers.

Fingers was most recognized for his handlebar mustache, but on the field, he helped define the closer position in baseball. Fingers spent just five seasons in Milwaukee in the early 1980s but made his mark in permanent ink. In 1981, Fingers won both the Cy Young Award and the American League MVP—the first pitcher to do so in 10 years. And since 1981, just two other closers have won both honors in the same year. In that magical season of 1981, Fingers gave up just nine runs the entire year. He saved 28 games for the Brewers in 1981 and finished with a remarkable 1.04 ERA.

But Fingers watched the Brewers' only World Series appearance from the dugout, since he missed the last month of the 1982 regular season and the entire postseason with a torn muscle in his elbow. In fact, most Brewers fans are convinced that Milwaukee would have won the World Series if Fingers was healthy.

Fingers was baseball's first modern-day closer—a guy who specialized in finishing games while protecting the lead. He made two of his seven All-Star appearances as a Brewer. Fingers finished his career with 341 saves—97 of those coming during his years in Milwaukee. He entered the Baseball Hall of Fame in 1992 and is one of four Brewers players to have his number retired.

WHAT ARE THE TOP FIVE HOME RUNS IN MILWAUKEE BASEBALL HISTORY?

50 One thing about baseball in Milwaukee— the home team has a flair for the dramatic. For instance, think of Dale Sveum hitting a walk-off, two-run home run to beat the Rangers on Easter Sunday for the Brewers' 12th straight win to open the season in 1987. That team that would be forever known as "Team Streak." But another big homer was hit on the road by Ned Yost, a light-hitting backup catcher, when he knocked out his one and only home run of the season and the biggest blast of his career in Boston to help the Brewers maintain their lead down the stretch of the 1982 season.

When Sixto Lezcano's name comes up, most Brewers fans immediately think of his walk-off grand slam on Opening Day in 1980. And Joe Adcock of the Milwaukee Braves is etched in baseball history for his part in ending one of the greatest games in big-league history on May 26, 1959. Pittsburgh's Harvey Haddix had pitched 12 perfect innings and retired 36 straight Braves before Adcock hit a home run in the 13th to end it. Technically, the homer was later changed to a double because Hank Aaron, who was on base at the time, ran off the field after the winning run crossed the plate and Adcock passed Aaron.

Hank Aaron hit his final home run in a Brewers uniform. It was home-run number 755, hit on July 20, 1976, at County Stadium against California Angels pitcher Dick Drago. And one of the more forgotten big Milwaukee moments came in the 1981 postseason, when Ted Simmons and Paul Molitor each hit home runs in an elimination game, Game 3 of the American League Divisional Series against the Yankees, to keep the series alive. More recently, Ryan Braun and Prince Fielder each knocked out walk-off home runs in the final week of the 2008 season to help the Brewers end a 26-year postseason drought. Braun's blast was a grand slam—just the seventh of the walk-off variety in Brewers history. But all these big flies just receive an honorable mention for the five biggest home runs in Milwaukee baseball history.

5. ROBIN YOUNT: OCTOBER 17, 1982, CARDINALS VERSUS BREWERS AT COUNTY STADIUM, MILWAUKEE, WISCONSIN

The Brewers led Game 5 of the 1982 World Series 3–2 in the seventh but needed some breathing room. Robin Yount allowed the capacity crowd at County Stadium to exhale with a vengeance. Yount went the other way against Bob Forsch with two outs to give the Brewers a 4–2 lead in the game and helping them to a 3–2 lead in the series. It was a huge home run, no question, but the Brewers would go on to drop back-to-back games in St. Louis and lose the World Series in seven games.

4. HANK AARON: SEPTEMBER 23, 1957, CARDINALS VERSUS BRAVES AT COUNTY STADIUM, MILWAUKEE, WISCONSIN

Hank Aaron hit 755 home runs in his Hall of Fame career, but this is the one he calls the biggest. It was the final week of the 1957 season, and the Braves were inching their way toward their first National League pennant in Milwaukee. The Braves had a comfortable lead down the stretch but were looking for the knockout punch. Hank Aaron delivered.

A capacity crowd of 40,926 filled County Stadium, and "the Hammer" made sure they left the park happy—*delirious* would be an even better word. The Cardinals and Braves played into the 11th inning when, at 11:34 p.m., St. Louis pitcher Billy Moffett grooved his first pitch to Aaron, and the young kid's powerful wrists did the rest. A line-drive home run over the center field fence won the game for the Braves and the pennant for Milwaukee.

3. RYAN BRAUN: SEPTEMBER 28, 2008, CUBS VERSUS BREWERS AT MILLER PARK, MILWAUKEE, WISCONSIN

The Brewers led the National League wild-card standings

by five and a half games on September 1 but managed to lose 11 of their next 14 games, and Manager Ned Yost was fired with two weeks to go in the regular season. If it wasn't for some clutch home runs during their final home stand, the Brewers' postseason drought would have continued. However, Ryan Braun, Prince Fielder, and Rickie Weeks all hit big shots in the final week of the season. Braun actually won two games with his bat—the biggest was the final game of the regular season.

The Brewers woke up on the last day of the season tied with the Mets for the National League wild card. New York was hosting the Florida Marlins in the final game played at Shea Stadium at the same time the Brewers were playing the Cubs. The Cubs had already clinched a spot in the playoffs by winning the NL Central but wanted nothing more than to spoil the Brewers' party. With C. C. Sabathia pitching another gem on short rest, the Brewers and Cubs were tied 1–1 in the bottom of the eighth. Offense was at a premium, especially for the Brewers, a team that was limping toward the finish line. With a man on, enter Ryan Braun, who wasted no time against Chicago reliever Bob Howry and crushed his first pitch into the left field stands, sending the Brewers faithful into another galaxy. The Brewers held on to win 3–1, and it was up to the Marlins to finish the job in New York. The sellout crowd of 45,299 stayed and watched the Marlins take care of business against the Mets on the video screen in center field, and the party was uncorked.

The Brewers had won the National League wild card thanks to Ryan Braun's big fly, ending 26 years of futility.

2. ROBIN YOUNT: OCTOBER 3, 1982, BREWERS VERSUS BALTIMORE AT MEMORIAL STADIUM, BALTIMORE, MARYLAND

The Brewers were in danger of one of the biggest collapses in baseball history. After leading the Orioles by four games with five to play, the Brewers had lost four straight—three in a row against Baltimore—while the Orioles had won four in a row. The two teams were now tied with just one game left to decide the American League East title. To make that hill even steeper to climb for Milwaukee, the O's sent future Hall of Famer Jim Palmer to the hill on that Sunday afternoon in Baltimore. But another future Hall of Famer set the tone; Robin Yount hit a first-inning home run off Palmer to right field that sucked the air out of the capacity crowd at Memorial Stadium. Before the afternoon was over, Yount had hit another home run and a triple in a game he'd later call the best of his career, leading the Brewers to a 10–2 win and clinching the AL East crown.

1. EDDIE MATHEWS: OCTOBER 6, 1957, YANKEES VERSUS BRAVES AT COUNTY STADIUM, MILWAUKEE, WISCONSIN

The biggest home run in Milwaukee history may not have been possible without Nippy Jones. The Yankees led the

1957 World Series 2–1 with Game 4 in Milwaukee. With the Yankees leading 5–4 in the 10th and in danger of taking a 3–1 series lead, the light-hitting Jones led off the home half of the frame. When New York pitcher Tommy Byrne bounced a pitch into the dirt, Jones reacted as if the ball had hit him on the shoe. The home plate umpire, Augie Donatelli, didn't buy it until Braves batboy Charlie Blossfield brought the ball in question to the ump. The ball clearly had the black smudge of shoe polish indicating that the ball had hit Jones. When Jones was awarded first base, it started a series of events that changed the course of the World Series. Jones would later score on a Johnny Logan double to tie the game 5–5.

Eddie Mathews was suffering through a terrible slump at the most important time of the year. The left-handed slugger was just 1 for 11 in the World Series when he stepped to the plate later in the 10th with Logan on second and two outs. Mathews could not even handle his own bat since it gave him blisters, so he borrowed some lumber from teammate Joe Adcock. The count was 2–2. Yankees right-hander Bob Grim fired a fastball at the belt, and Mathews crushed it: a two-run, walk-off home run just in front of the right field bleachers. It was the only postseason home run in Mathews's Hall of Fame career. The final score was Braves 7, Yankees 5, evening up the series 2–2. Eddie Mathews's home run in Game 4 was the turning point in the series. The Braves would take two of the next three games, both wins by pitcher Lew Burdette, wrapping up the one and only World Series title in Wisconsin history.

WHAT'S THE BEST TRADE IN MILWAUKEE BASEBALL HISTORY?

51 Unlike football, a midseason trade in baseball can be a difference-maker. It's so true for the Milwaukee Braves and Milwaukee Brewers. The Braves won the National League pennant in 1957 and 1958. The Brewers made the playoffs in 1981, 1982, and 2008. Each time, the teams could point to a big trade that made playing October baseball possible.

Terrific trades aren't limited to just those five playoff clubs in those particular years. In fact, many of the great trades in Milwaukee baseball history laid the groundwork years before to help those clubs reach the postseason. In 1976, the Brewers traded George Scott and Bernie Carbo to the Red Sox for a first baseman known more as a contact hitter than a slugger in Cecil Cooper. In December 1977, the Brewers sent pitcher Jim Slaton to the Tigers for outfielder Ben Ogilvie, who instantly became a staple in left field for Milwaukee. Slaton, meanwhile, missed Milwaukee so much that he spent just one season in Detroit before returning to the Cream City, signing as a free agent in 1978.

Speaking of the 1982 Brewers, Don Sutton is considered to be the final piece of their pennant-winning puzzle. The future Hall of Famer was acquired by Milwaukee in September for cash and three players to be named later. Those three players turned out to be Kevin Bass, Frank DiPino, and Mike Madden. Sutton went 4–1 in seven starts to finish the regular season and then won Game 3 of the ALCS, an elimination game, to help the Brewers stay alive and start their amazing three-game run to the American League title.

Even those great trades fail to make the top three. Following are the best of the best trades in Milwaukee baseball history.

3. BRAVES ACQUIRE RED SCHOENDIENST

On June 15, 1957, the Milwaukee Braves made the move that put them over the hump from pretender to contender. They sent three players to the New York Giants for second baseman Red Schoendienst. He not only solidified the Braves infield, but also hit .310 and helped the Braves win back-to-back National League pennants and the only World Series title in Milwaukee baseball history in 1957.

2. BREWERS ACQUIRE C. C. SABATHIA

Brewers general manager Doug Melvin said the Brewers were "going for it," and by that, he meant mortgaging part of the future for the present. Matt LaPorta, Zach Jackson,

155

Rob Bryson, and a player to be named later were the price set by the Indians for C. C. Sabathia. No question it was a risky move for potentially a short-term investment, but it was a gamble that paid off in a big way. All Sabathia did was win 11 of his 17 Brewers starts, losing just two. He became just the second pitcher in the last nine decades to win his first nine decisions following a midseason change of uniforms. Sabathia led the Brewers with seven complete games and three shutouts, and he had a minuscule 1.65 ERA as the Brewers went 14–3 in his starts. Sabathia's final win came on the last day of the regular season, as he beat the Cubs 3–1, helping the Brewers to clinch the NL wild card. Sabathia was named the Brewers' 2008 MVP, as well as their Most Valuable Pitcher. All of this was after arriving in Milwaukee in the terrific trade of July 7, 2008.

1. BREWERS ACQUIRE ROLLIE FINGERS, TED SIMMONS, AND PETE VUCKOVICH

Brewers general manager Harry Dalton earns a hat trick here. On December 12, 1980, Dalton made the best trade in Milwaukee baseball history, sending pitchers Dave LaPoint and Larry Sorensen, outfielder Sixto Lezcano, and minor-league hotshot David Green to the Cardinals for catcher Ted Simmons, pitcher Pete Vuckovich, and closer Rollie Fingers. To think that some of the Brewers brass did not want to make the deal, fearing that giving away David Green was too steep a price to pay! The trade was eventually made at the winter meetings in Dallas, and the Brewers received the next two Cy Young Award–winners as well as the American League MVP in 1981. Fingers won both the Cy Young and the MVP in 1981, going 6–3 with 28 saves and a 1.04 ERA. Vuckovich went 14–4 in 1981, and in 1982, he won the Cy Young Award, going 18–6 and helping the Brewers to the AL pennant. Fingers saved 29 more games in 1982 before getting shut down in September with a sore arm. As for Simmons, he provided pop from both sides of the plate, hitting 14 home runs and driving in 61 runs in 1981. He bettered those numbers in 1982, clubbing 23 home runs to go with 97 RBI. Three key cogs in one trade helped the Brewers to a playoff berth in 1981 and an American League pennant in 1982.

WHAT'S THE WORST TRADE IN MILWAUKEE BASEBALL HISTORY?

52 All in all, Milwaukee baseball has made more good trades than bad. There isn't a Lou Brock for Ernie Broglio on this list. Some deals have been a wash, like Scott Podsednik and Luis Vizcaino for Carlos Lee of the White Sox in December 2004. Or even Carlos Lee and Nelson Cruz to the Rangers for Francisco Cordero, Kevin Mench, Laynce Nix, and a minor leaguer. The Gary Sheffield trade to San Diego fails to make this list for the simple reason that Sheffield wanted out of Milwaukee in the worst way, and there was nothing the Brewers could do. Their hands were tied, so they had to move him. They received serviceable big leaguers in Ricky Bones, Jose Valentin, and Matt Mieske. There's also the forgettable Dante Bichette trade to the Rockies for Kevin Reimer in 1992. All Bichette did was turn himself into an MVP candidate hitting in the light air of Colorado. Reimer just hit lightly (.249, 13 HR, 60 RBI) in his lone season in Milwaukee.

Even though some still rip the Brewers for trading Richie Sexson to the Diamondbacks for what seemed like half of

Arizona's roster, the Sexson trade served its purpose to help the Brewers stay competitive until their young guys (J. J. Hardy, Prince Fielder, Corey Hart, and Rickie Weeks) made it through the minor-league system. That's not to say there haven't been any duds. Here are three deals for which Milwaukee baseball fans wish they had a mulligan.

3. DARRYL PORTER AND JIM COLBURN TO ROYALS FOR JIM WOHLFORD, JAMIE QUIRK, AND PLAYER TO BE NAMED LATER

On December 6, 1976, the Brewers sent starting catcher Darrell Porter and a solid starter in Jim Colburn to the Royals. In return, they received a journeyman outfielder, a light-hitting DH, and a player to be named later. Porter went on to play 11 years with the Royals, Cardinals, and Rangers and made the All-Star team three times after getting traded. He was the dagger in this deal, since he was the MVP of the 1982 World Series for the Cardinals when they beat the Brewers in seven games. Colburn, meanwhile, won 18 games for Kansas City in his first and only full season with the Royals.

Jim Wohlford played three seasons in Milwaukee—his best was in 1977, when he hit .248 to go with 17 stolen bases. Jamie Quirk played 93 games in 1977, his only season in Milwaukee, when he hit three home runs to go with 13 RBI. The only thing that saved this trade from becoming one of the all-time worst was that the player to be named later turned out to be Bob McClure. The crafty left-hander spent almost 10 seasons in Milwaukee and was a key cog in the rotation, winning 12 games in the magical year of 1982.

2. GORMAN THOMAS, ERNIE COMACHO, AND JAMIE EASTERLY FOR RICK MANNING AND RICK WAITS

What have you done for me lately? That question can be applied to Gorman Thomas, who in 1982 slugged 39 home runs and drove in 112 runs for the Brewers. When Stormin' Gorman struggled out of the gate the next season, batting .183 with just five home runs into June, Thomas was traded to the Indians, along with pitchers Ernie Comacho and Jamie Easterly. In return, the Brewers received Rick Manning and Rick Waits. Manning never hit better than .254 in his five seasons, and he's best known in Milwaukee for his role in helping end Paul Molitor's 39-game hitting streak. Manning drove in the game-winning run in the 10th inning to beat his old team, the Indians, with Molitor on deck. Manning suffered the rare indignity of being booed at home after a game-winning hit. Was it fair Manning got the blame for Molitor's streak being snapped? No, Molitor was 0 for 4 at that point and had his chances earlier in the game. It still didn't stop thousands of fans voicing their displeasure with Manning.

The other principles in the deal did not amount to much. Waits had a nice three-year run as a starter when he won 42 games for the Indians from 1978 to 1980; however, he worked out of the bullpen for the Brewers. He pitched 150 nondescript innings for Milwaukee over his three seasons with the team. Left-hander Jamie Easterly pitched for five seasons in Cleveland and was a solid option out of the bullpen. Ernie Comacho lasted eight seasons with four teams as a right-handed reliever.

Most important, the act of trading Thomas ripped the heart out of the Brewers fan base. Thomas was a guy whom fans grew up with. He was one of the few worthwhile players to come to town from the Seattle Pilots when they moved to Milwaukee in 1970. Thomas was the Pilots' first-round draft pick in 1969 and made his big-league debut with the Brewers in 1973. He was a rough-and-tumble, fearless outfielder who played with his heart on his sleeve. When he was traded from Milwaukee, a piece of the Brewers left with him. The Brewers then went 26 years without a postseason appearance.

1. CAL ELDRED AND JOSE VALENTIN TO THE WHITE SOX FOR JOHN SNYDER AND JAMIE NAVARRO

On paper, this trade in January 2000 doesn't look like much. It looks like one man's trash for another man's trash. However, the Brewers' "trash" turned into treasure.

Eldred rekindled the magic he had in his rookie season; he went 10–2 for the White Sox. Jose Valentin hit 25 home runs, which are included in his 68 extra-base hits in his first season in Chicago. After signing again with the White Sox, Valentin hit 25 or more home runs in each of the following four seasons. Valentin also had value as an outfielder—something that the Brewers never fully realized. Plus, he was smart. Drew Olson, the Brewers beat reporter for the *Milwaukee Journal* and then the *Milwaukee Journal-Sentinel* for more than a decade, said of Valentin, "He had the best baseball IQ of anyone I covered." As for Navarro and Snyder—Navarro went 0–5 in his first five starts of 2000 and was released at the end of April, and Snyder went 3–10 in his one and only season in Milwaukee.

WAS FIRING NED YOST THE RIGHT OR WRONG MOVE?

53 The Ned Yost firing was intended to shake up the Milwaukee Brewers' clubhouse in the final weeks of the 2008 season, but it first sent shock waves through Brewer nation. Fans questioned the move so late in the season. Granted, the Brewers were in a tailspin, having lost 11 of 14 games to start September, but this was the same manager who had led his team to 20 wins in August. The Brewers led the wild card by five and a half games at the start of September only to watch the lead disappear two weeks later, which triggered the move.

General Manager Doug Melvin said the tipping point was when Yost didn't have any answers for his club's recent losing streak. "I'm not sure I have all the answers. I'm not sure this is the right one either," Melvin said at the news conference to announce the move. "I'm going to turn the managerial position over to [third base coach] Dale Sveum and hope we can kick-start a club we feel has a lot of talent."

The move to fire Yost was surprising because of the timing. The season was 92.6 percent complete. Two weeks remained. If you were going to make a change, wouldn't a midyear move have been more effective?

Although he said it was a group decision, it appeared Brewers owner Mark Attanasio was the trigger man. Of course, Doug Melvin played the part of the good solider and took the hit as the man who made the "final decision." But if you had $90 million invested in a product, wouldn't you have the final say? It was a bold move, a gutsy move by Attanasio, but was it in the best interest of the ball club?

If Ned Yost had led the Brewers to the playoffs, he would have had to be brought back to manage the next season. By firing him with 12 games left, you put the onus on Sveum to try to snap a playoff drought that had lasted more than a quarter-century. If Sveum fails to get the Brewers into the postseason, you fire him, too, and start fresh in 2009, when expectations will be lower since the team lost its top two pitchers. But Doug Melvin did say when he traded for C. C. Sabathia that the Brewers were "going for it," and by making the change at manager, the perception was consistent with that notion.

It was a questionable decision to fire Yost with less than two weeks to go in the regular season. If management wanted to get rid of him, why not fire him when the team was 20–24 in May, after getting swept in Boston? Plus, Yost deserved to see the season through. He endured a 106-loss season in his first year in Milwaukee. He had to play prospects that were not necessarily major-league ready simply because they were the best option. Yes, Yost was loyal to a fault, but he still had the club tied for the wild card with 12 games to go.

Agree or disagree with the move, the Brewers won six of their final seven games to make the playoffs. But their postseason run lasted just four games as the Phillies defeated the Crew three games to one in the National League Divisional Series. Sveum led the team to the playoffs and was promptly fired after the Brewers were eliminated. Would Yost have managed the team deeper into the postseason? Who knows? But he should have been given the chance to finish what he had started.

WAS STARTING JEFF SUPPAN IN GAME 4 A MISTAKE?

54

The Brewers' first trip to the playoffs in 26 years ended too soon in 2008. It lasted just four games. The Phillies delivered the knockout punch on Sunday, October 5, blasting four home runs off Brewers pitching—three of them off starter Jeff Suppan. Some Brewers fans are still livid that Suppan got the start in Game 4, but Dale Sveum made the right call.

Suppan had been struggling. He was just 0–3 in five starts in September, with a gaudy 8.44 ERA. That included a five-inning stint in which he gave up just one run against the Cubs on the final weekend of the regular season. Brewers interim manager Dale Sveum didn't have many options. Yovani Gallardo had started Game 1, so he would have to pitch on short rest. Gallardo had just two starts under his belt since tearing up his knee May 1, which required surgery. Manny Parra hit a wall as a starter late in the regular season and was sent to the bullpen when Sveum took over. Seth McClung was a possibility, but he had pitched two innings in Philadelphia, as well.

For some reason or another, the Phillies had Suppan figured out. He was 3–6 lifetime against Philadelphia entering the 2008 postseason, and his 6.13 ERA was his highest against any National League opponent. But what Suppan had was postseason experience.

When Suppan signed a four-year contract worth $42 million on Christmas Eve 2006, the veteran right-hander was fresh off a dominating postseason. As a member of the St. Louis Cardinals, he was the Most Valuable Player of the National League Championship Series, giving up just one run against the Mets in 15 innings pitched. Suppan then helped St. Louis sweep Detroit to win the World Series. He was a proven big-game pitcher. Suppan was rewarded with the then-largest contract in Brewers history. One of the reasons the Brewers signed Suppan in the first place was to pitch in big moments like Game 4.

Phillies shortstop Jimmy Rollins set the tone leading off in Game 4 by hitting a 3–2 pitch into the right field bleachers off Suppan. However, the wheels fell off in the third inning. With Shane Victorino on third with two outs, Suppan intentionally walked Ryan Howard. Why not? Howard was the hottest hitter in the big leagues at the end of the regular season, and the next man up, Pat Burrell, was 1 for 9 in the NLDS to that point and was hitting just .238 against right-handers that season. Suppan was one pitch from getting out of the jam and keeping the game 1–0. Unfortunately, his 2–2 pitch was an 88-mile-an-hour fastball that Burrell crushed for a three-run home run—the first of two in the game for Burrell. It helped the Phillies beat the Brewers 6–2 to win the series three games to one. On his decision to start Suppan, Sveum had no regrets. "I don't think there was any question of starting [Suppan] today," Sveum said. "He got the rest he usually does, and with one pitch difference, he's out of the inning and it might be a different game. There was never a doubt that he was going to be our fourth-game starter."

Hindsight has Lasik. You can argue that Gallardo came in for Suppan and pitched one-hit ball over three innings, but the Phillies had a 5–0 cushion at that point. Though he had struggled in September, Suppan had been brilliant in August, going 5–0 with a 3.00 ERA. Above all, Suppan had big-game experience and was signed as a free agent because he pitched in the playoffs in three separate seasons. Sometimes, the better team wins a game and a series. In 2008, the Phillies were the better team, and more importantly, the hotter team, no matter who had started in Game 4.

WHO DO BREWERS FANS LOVE TO HATE MORE?

55 Brewers fans love to hate former manager Ned Yost. Even when he was winning, Yost was a lightning rod for criticism, both inside and outside the ballpark. Radio talk-show hosts should have written Yost a thank-you card for the material he supplied them during his nearly six seasons in Milwaukee. It's strange to think that a man who helped turn the Brewers around would be such a target. After all, Yost led the Brewers to their first non-losing season in 13 years in 2005, and two years later, to their first winning season in 15 years, but Yost was the fuel that lit the fire. Sure, he was occasionally condescending to the media and sometimes came across as gruff during news conferences, but it was hard to understand the fans' venom for Yost.

Like most managers, he was second-guessed; however, for the first time in 2008, the average fan regularly saw exactly what reporters endured after games, thanks to Fox Sports Net airing his postgame news conferences in their entirety. Yost questioned reporters constantly, he was sarcastic and cranky at times, and it was obvious that he did not enjoy his daily dealings with the media.

However, Yost got a bum rap. He was publicly loyal to his players, and never did he throw one of his guys under the bus, though he had plenty of opportunities to do so. Some would say he was too loyal—for example, sticking with Rickie Weeks in the leadoff spot. Maybe it's because fans think they could do his job. Think about it. The average fan would never be able to call plays for the Packers or even draw up an in-bounds pass for the Bucks, but everyone and their mother thinks they could skipper the Brewers. Yost once told a reporter that the criticism was part of the game, admitting his own mother would question some of his moves. However, Yost said the fan involvement showed the passion of Brewers fans, and he made a terrific point when he said that when he started as manager in 2003, no one cared who was batting leadoff.

There is a group of people that makes Brewers fans blood boil even more than Ned Yost. It's the Chicago Cubs. Hands down, they are Brewers Enemy No. 1. Separated by just 90 miles, the two teams are quickly generating a rivalry that could match any in the big leagues. The Cubs have been a thorn in the side of the Brewers. In 2007, Aramis Ramirez's walk-off home run at Wrigley Field off Francisco Cordero was a sign of what was to come for the first-place Brewers: the Cubs would win the Central, and Milwaukee would fade down the stretch. In the middle of the pennant race, September 18, 2008, the Brewers and closer Salomon Torres blew a four-run lead with two outs in the ninth, also at Wrigley Field. The Cubs would again go on to win the Central; the Brewers would win the NL wild card. In fact, when the Cubs were swept by the Dodgers in the opening round of the 2008 playoffs and the Brewers lost their best-of-five series in four games to the Phillies, J. J. Hardy smiled when asked about the Cubs. "We lasted one day longer," said Hardy.

It's the fans that make the rivalry so spirited. After Miller Park opened in 2001, the only games that were sure sell-outs were those against the Cubs. You see, it was easier (and cheaper) for Cubs fans to get tickets to see their team play at Miller Park than at Wrigley Field. Miller Park quickly became known to Cubs fans as "Wrigley North." When the Brewers became competitive, the team held a ticket promotion called "Take Back Miller Park," which gave local fans a special deal for buying tickets to see the Brewers host the Cubs.

Major League Baseball is catching on to the Cubs–Brewers rivalry. In 2008, the Brewers opened the season at Wrigley Field and closed the regular season at home hosting the Cubs. In between, the two teams played in a playoff atmosphere each time they took the field against one another. The only thing better for Brewers fans would be if Ned Yost somehow, someday, came back to manage the Cubs. Then Brewers fans would be able to root against both things they love to hate. But for now, Ned Yost is out of sight, out of mind in Milwaukee, leaving the Cubs as the one thing Brewers fans love to hate.

WHICH IS THE BETTER LOGO, THE BALL AND GLOVE OR THE BARLEY "M"?

56 Do you know who Tom Meindel is? If you are a Brewers fan, you should. He is the creator of the coolest logo in team history, the ball in glove. Back in 1977, Meindel was an art education student at UW–Eau Claire and beat out 2,000 other entries in a contest to create a new logo for the Brewers. To the untrained eye, the glove looks like a regular glove holding a ball. But just like Kramer did on that old episode of *Seinfeld,* when the eyes are relaxed, the real vision comes out. The simple yet unique design features the lowercase letters *m* and *b* holding a baseball. Meindel's reward for designing the Brewers logo was $2,000. Talk about bang for your buck. That $2,000 investment gave the Brewers their logo for 15 years, from 1978 to 1993. The design was so popular that it's had a renaissance in recent years. The Brewers have worn throwback uniforms one day a week during home stands as a tip of the cap, so to speak, to their glory days.

The Brewers' modern-day logo, the barley under the cursive *M,* is a nice touch and a much-needed improvement over the worst logo in baseball history, the intertwined *M* and *B* with crossed baseball bats of the mid-1990s. The team's original logo, the barrel man, was cool, but there's nothing cooler than the ball-in-glove logo the Brewers wore in the 1980s.

The kicker to all this is that Meindel never received any royalties after designing the logo—just the $2,000 for winning the contest. In fact, later in life, he worked for a printing company that used his Brewers logo on merchandise, and he had to pay royalties to the team and Major League Baseball to use the logo that he designed.

WHICH IS THE MOST UNSUNG BASEBALL TEAM IN MILWAUKEE HISTORY?

57 Everyone talks in glowing terms about the 1957 Braves and 1982 Brewers, but few fans even mention the '58 Braves and '81 Brewers. Both teams made the playoffs and yet both teams struggle for the proper respect they deserve. Which begs the question, which club is more overlooked?

THE 1958 BRAVES

Coming off a World Series title, the 1958 Braves made it back to the Fall Classic and again faced the New York Yankees. The Braves won three of the first four games of the series, meaning all they had to do to repeat as champions was win one of the final three games of the best-of-seven series. However, the Yankees ripped off three straight wins, including the final two in Milwaukee, to break the hearts of Milwaukee baseball fans. The Braves simply stopped hitting, they scored more runs in Game 2 (13) than in the other six games combined and hit just .250 as a team for the series. The collapse wasted a brilliant series for Warren Spahn. The 37-year-old left-hander out dueled fellow Hall of Famer Whitey Ford for wins in Game 1 and Game 4. Spahn came back on two days rest to pitch Game 6 and pitched another gem. He held the Yankees to just two runs through nine innings before the Yankees finally broke through in the 10th, scoring twice and then holding on to win 4–3. The Yankees became just the second team in major-league history to come back from a 3–1 deficit to win a World Series, and the first since the Pirates did it 33 years prior in 1925.

THE 1981 BREWERS

The Brewers of 1981 are a forgotten team. Maybe it was because of the strike-shortened season. Maybe it was the team's exit in the first divisional round in playoff history. Whatever the reason, the 1981 Brewers are the redheaded stepchild of the franchise, and that should not be. The 1981 Brewers club was the first Milwaukee baseball team since the 1958 Braves to make it to the playoffs. The Brewers won the second half of the strike-shortened season and qualified for the first divisional round of the playoffs, where they faced the New York Yankees in a best-of-five series for the right to move on to the ALCS.

The Brewers lost the opening two games at County Stadium but managed to win Game 3 and Game 4 at Yankee Stadium to force the fifth and deciding game in

New York. Gorman Thomas put the Brewers up 1–0 with a solo home run in the second, and Milwaukee added another run on a Cecil Cooper sacrifice fly in the third. However, Brewers starter Moose Haas could not hold the lead, and the Yankees turned the tide with a four-run fourth inning. The big blows were back-to-back homers: first, a two-run blast by "Mr. October" himself, Reggie Jackson, to tie the game, and then a solo shot by Oscar Gamble to give New York the lead for good. The Yankees went on to win Game 5 by a score of 7–3 and win the series 3–2. The Yankees would eventually lose to the Dodgers in the 1981 World Series.

THE VERDICT

The 1981 Brewers were such an afterthought that they averaged just over 30,000 fans a game in their two home playoff games at County Stadium. In fact, the stadium was half-full when only 26,295 showed up for Game 2—an embarrassing figure. The playoff format was unique that year, because the baseball strike forced the playoffs to add an extra round, but it's incredible to think that a playoff game would fail to sell out, even in 1981—especially since it was the first playoff appearance in Brewers history.

The 1958 Braves do not get as much respect as the 1957 club for the simple reason that they failed to win the World Series. In reality, the 1958 club came up a game short of the 1957 team, but they are just one of three Milwaukee

177

baseball teams to play in the World Series. As years go by, however, the 1958 team is now given a certain degree a respect, since it is usually grouped with the 1957 champs—much like the 1997 Packers are grouped with the 1996 team as the two teams that "went to back-to-back Super Bowls," even though one won and one lost.

Not many fans group the 1981 and 1982 Brewers teams together, although they should. The 1981 team fails to get the proper respect, now *and* then. The team did win 62 of 109 games played in the regular season and was the first Brewers team to qualify for postseason play, even if it was in a manufactured divisional round because of the strike. Granted, the 1981 Brewers are not at the same level as the 1982 Brewers, but they deserve better. Since the 1981 team set the table for the pennant-winning club that followed a year later. The 1981 Brewers are definitely more unsung than the 1958 Braves.

THE BUCKS

WHO MAKES THE BUCKS' ALL-TIME TEAM?

58 POINT GUARD

The Bucks have called Milwaukee home since 1968. Over the years, hundreds of players have worn either the forest green and red, the purple and green, or the current deep red and green of the Bucks colors. Who's the best of the Bucks? At point guard, it boils down to two players, Sam Cassell and Oscar Robertson. On the surface, it's almost preposterous to think that Cassell could hold a candle to "the Big O," but if you look at the numbers, it's closer than you'd think. Cassell averaged 19 points, seven assists, and four rebounds a game during his five seasons in Milwaukee, while Robertson's numbers with the Bucks read 16 points, 7.5 assists, and five rebounds a game. The big difference between the two was winning games.

The Bucks won 54 percent of their games with Cassell in the driver's seat. They made a memorable run to the Eastern Conference Finals in 2001 before losing to the Sixers in seven games, but that's as close as they ever got. In all, Milwaukee went to the playoffs in three of Cassell's four full seasons in Milwaukee, losing in the first round in their other two trips to the playoffs with him.

This is where Robertson blows Cassell away. The Bucks won division titles all four years that Robertson was the Bucks' point guard. Milwaukee won its one and only NBA championship with Robertson at the controls in 1971 and made it back to the finals in 1974. "The Big O" set the Bucks' single-season assist record in their championship season, at 8.5 a game, and helped his club to 20 straight victories that year—an NBA record that stood for more than 35 years. Remarkably, Sam Cassell won more NBA championship rings than Oscar Robertson (two with Houston and one with Boston), but on the All-Time Bucks team, "the Big O" is the starter at point guard.

59 SHOOTING GUARD

There's no question that Ray Allen could shoot the basketball. Allen averaged more than 20 points a game in four straight seasons, and he finished his time in Milwaukee averaging 19.6 points per game—almost three points a game better than Sidney Moncrief. The difference between the two players was defense. Moncrief was a defensive stopper. He won the NBA's Defensive Player of the Year Award twice and made the All-NBA Defensive Team for four straight seasons. Moncrief was a five-time All Star, compared to Allen's three All-Star selections as a Buck.

Moncrief's defense led to Bucks victories. Milwaukee made the playoffs in all 10 of Moncrief's seasons, winning seven division titles. The Bucks averaged 52 wins a season during the Moncrief era. In comparison, Allen led the Bucks to three appearances in the playoffs in his six full seasons in Milwaukee.

Sidney Moncrief is one of the best all-around players in Bucks history, and it's a travesty that "Sir Sid" is not yet in the Hall of Fame. Moncrief ranks third on the Bucks' all-time scoring list but ranks No. 1 as the Bucks' best shooting guard of all time.

60 CENTER

The strongest position in the Bucks starting five is center. The best big man in Bucks history is a choice between two Hall of Famers, Bob Lanier and Kareem Abdul-Jabbar. Bob Lanier was a winner. Acquired from the Pistons for Kent Benson and a first-round pick, "the Dobber" gave Milwaukee a much-needed veteran presence, bad knees and all. The Bucks averaged 53 wins a year and won division titles in each of Lanier's five seasons in Milwaukee. Lanier made such an impact in such a short period of time that the Bucks retired his number 16 even before his original team, the Pistons, did so. Lanier was an outstanding talent, but he plays second fiddle to the best big man in Bucks history.

Winning a coin flip never paid such huge dividends. In the spring of 1969, the worst teams in each conference, the Bucks and Suns, flipped a coin to see which team would earn the rights to pick first in the NBA draft. The winner would win the right to draft Lew Alcindor, the best college basketball player in the country. Phoenix called heads, and the coin turned up tails. Milwaukee selected the big man from UCLA, and Alcindor did not disappoint.

Lew Alcindor was the NBA's Rookie of the Year in 1970 and was a three-time winner of the league's Most Valuable Player Award (1970–1971, 1971–1972, and 1973–1974). Most importantly, Alcindor was the big reason why the Bucks won their one and only NBA championship in the franchise's third (Alcindor's second) season in the league.

Alcindor would eventually change his name to Kareem Abdul-Jabbar and would leave Milwaukee in a trade to the Lakers in 1975. But in his six seasons in Milwaukee, he averaged a team-record 30.6 points per game. With help from his "sky-hook," Abdul-Jabbar scored 14,211 points and grabbed 7,161 rebounds as a member of the Bucks—both all-time franchise records. Abdul-Jabbar also holds team records in field goals made (5,902), field goals attempted (10,787), and field-goal percentage (54.7 percent). He was elected to the Hall of Fame in 1995. Abdul-Jabbar is the only player in Bucks history to have worn the number 33. The number was retired in 1993. Like Lanier, he's one of the few players to have his number retired by more than one team (the Lakers retired Abdul-Jabbar's number 33 in 1989). He was named one of the NBA's 50 greatest players during the league's 50th anniversary season of 1996–1997.

61 SMALL FORWARD

When determining the Bucks all-time small forward, it's a three-man competition between Marques Johnson, Glenn Robinson and Bob Dandridge. Throw out the final year that Bob Dandridge played in Milwaukee—it was a farewell season, as he returned to finish his career where he started. So the numbers being considered for Dandridge are for his first eight seasons in Milwaukee.

As the Bucks grew as a franchise, Bob Dandridge grew as a player. He was drafted in the fourth round, three rounds after Milwaukee selected Lew Alcindor, and the two gave the Bucks an instant one-two punch in the front-court. Dandridge made the NBA All-Star team three times in Milwaukee, and led the Bucks to the playoffs in his first five seasons. In those first eight seasons, Dandridge averaged almost 19 points and 7.4 rebounds a game.

Glenn Robinson could score as he ranks only behind Kareem Abdul-Jabbar on the Bucks' all-time scoring list. Even though "the Big Dog" finished his Milwaukee career with a better scoring average (21.14) than Marques Johnson (21.0) and Bob Dandridge (18.8), Robinson finishes third on this list, since he was one-dimensional—he was just a scorer.

So the debate is between Dandridge and Johnson. The thing Marques Johnson did best was shoot field goals at a high percentage. Johnson played seven seasons for the Bucks. He shot at least 50 percent from the field in all seven seasons. Johnson finished his time in Milwaukee shooting 53 percent from the field, ranking him behind only Abdul-Jabbar and Bob Lanier in the franchise's record books. Johnson played in four All-Star Games, one more than Dandridge as a Buck and was named as a starter twice. He was named to the first team All-NBA in 1978–1979 and to the second team in both the 1979–1980 and 1980–1981 seasons. Johnson could also handle the ball as a big man. He famously coined the phrase "point forward," giving himself that position title in the playoffs in 1983. Plus, you have to love a guy who became a role-player in Hollywood after his playing days ended. Johnson appeared in movies like *White Men Can't Jump, Blue Chips,* and *Forget Paris.*

Johnson scored more than Dandridge and almost as much as Robinson, plus Johnson shot a better percentage and was widely regarded around the NBA as one of the best players in the league. Marques Johnson gets the nod on the all-time Bucks team as the starting small forward.

62 POWER FORWARD

To find the best Bucks power forward, you have to look beyond the numbers. First of all, throw out the final season that Terry Cummings

185

played for the Bucks. It was the 1995–1996 season, and Cummings was in the twilight of his career, backing up a hotshot named Vin Baker. Cummings came off the bench that season and managed to bring his stellar career stats down a few pegs. For argument's sake, we will look at Cummings's prime years in Milwaukee (1984–1989) against Baker's four seasons with the Bucks (1993–1997).

Cummings averaged 21.7 points and 8.3 rebounds a game in his five seasons versus Baker's 18.3 points and 9.5 rebounds. Yes, Baker did average a double-double twice in his four seasons—something Cummings never did in Milwaukee—and Baker went to the All-Star Game three times as a Buck, while Cummings went twice. The question is this: would you rather have a good player on a great team or a good player on a terrible team? Most would pick the good player on the great club, and that means taking Terry Cummings. The Bucks made the playoffs in all five of his prime years in Milwaukee, winning two Central Division titles. Baker's Bucks averaged just 28 victories in his four seasons and never made the playoffs. Sure, Cummings's Bucks had other options, like Sidney Moncrief and Paul Pressey, but that makes his numbers even more impressive. Cummings was still able to score and rack up his rebounding totals in the context of winning, which is something Baker can't say. That's why Terry Cummings gets the vote as the Bucks' best power forward.

63 COACH

Karl, Nelson, and Costello sounds like a law firm, but those three names represent the three most successful head coaches in Bucks history. You can make a valid argument that both George Karl and Don Nelson are more beloved than Larry Costello, and that's probably true, but the only coach to win an NBA title for Milwaukee is Costello. The three had similar success in the regular season. Nelson won 61 percent of his games during his 11 seasons in Milwaukee—the best winning percentage of the three. The separation comes in the postseason. Larry Costello is the only Bucks head coach with a winning playoff record, 37–23. He helped the Bucks make it to the finals twice, in 1971 and 1974. Granted, it's easier to get to the finals when Oscar Robertson is your point guard and Kareem Abdul-Jabbar is your center, but the fact is that Costello did it and won it all, while the other two did not. This makes Costello the all-time coach of the Bucks.

WHO KILLED THE TURN-OF-THE-CENTURY BUCKS?

64

The Bucks came within a Glenn "Big Dog" Robinson jump shot of making it to the NBA Finals in 2001. It was a magical run that showed basketball fans around the state just how exciting the NBA playoffs could be. However, the run was short-lived. Robinson missed that jumper, and the Bucks lost Game 5 in Philadelphia and wound up losing the series in seven games to the 76ers. With the key parts in place, Bucks fans geared themselves up for another playoff run the following season. It never happened. The question is why?

The biggest change to the team came in the final week of October 2001, when the Bucks traded Scott Williams to the Suns and then signed Anthony Mason to a four-year contract worth $21 million. Williams was a glue guy, a role-player who was an active ingredient in promoting good team chemistry. Mason was the opposite. He liked his touches in offensive sets, which took away shots from the "Big Three" of Sam Cassell, Ray Allen, and Robinson. The team struggled on the floor and off. The Bucks went from just missing out on the NBA Finals to missing the playoffs completely, thanks to a colossal collapse down the stretch of the regular season. Despite playing in one of the NBA's smallest markets, the Bucks ranked in the top five in payroll. Head Coach George Karl blamed himself. Karl was the guy who pushed the owner, Senator Herb Kohl, to acquire Mason, and the move backfired. Karl was making $7 million a year and yet could not figure out the right buttons to push, so his team failed.

After missing the playoffs in 2002, the Bucks traded Robinson, and then on February 20, 2003, they traded Allen to Seattle for one of Karl's favorite players, Gary Payton, as part of a five-player deal. Allen was the most popular Buck at the time, and trading him away sent shock waves through the city. What made the trade even worse was that Payton had just a few months left on his contract and left Milwaukee after that season. Cassell was traded to the Timberwolves shortly thereafter.

Who's to blame for a team that won 52 games one year and missed the playoffs the next? In fact, since their run to the Eastern Conference Finals in 2001, the Bucks haven't won a playoff series. You can point the finger at George Karl, since he wanted Mason and Payton. You can blame General Manager Ernie Grunfeld, who pulled the trigger on the deals. But the ultimate decision-maker is the Bucks' owner, Senator Herb Kohl. It was he who provided the money for one of the top payrolls in the league, and yet he only got to enjoy one serious run in the playoffs. It was his seal of approval that was needed for any of the major moves to be made. Granted, no one wants to win more than the good senator, and give him credit for thinking outside the box; however, sometimes it's best to play the hand you have. Acquiring Anthony Mason was the first big mistake, which ultimately led to the unraveling of a terrific core of players. The players play the game, but if Bucks fans want to blame someone for the mess made after 2001, they can blame Senator Kohl—in the end, the buck stops with him.

WHAT'S THE BEST TRADE IN BUCKS HISTORY?

65 Over the years, the Bucks have pulled off some blockbuster trades—some good, some not so good. The Bucks have always been bold—they once traded the NBA's all-time leading scorer to the Lakers. The Kareem Abdul-Jabbar trade in 1975 was one that was both good and bad for the Bucks. There's no denying the trade had to be made. The disgruntled superstar wanted out of Milwaukee. However, the Bucks brass was shrewd enough to get four players for Abdul-Jabbar, including Brian Winters and Junior Bridgeman, in the deal. The shakeup trade in September 1984 was a pretty good one, too. The Bucks sent aging Marques Johnson, Junior Bridgeman, and Harvey Catchings to the Clippers in exchange for Terry Cummings, Craig Hodges, and Ricky Pierce. The Bucks have also been active using the draft. On June 7, 1977, they traded Swen Nater to Buffalo for the third pick in the draft, which was used to select Marques Johnson. Those three deals receive special mention but fall short of making it into the top three trades in Bucks history.

3. KENT BENSON AND A FIRST-ROUND DRAFT PICK TO THE DETROIT PISTONS FOR BOB LANIER, 1980

This was a huge deal that pushed the Bucks over the top, getting them the big man they lacked since the Abdul-Jabbar trade. Lanier led the Bucks to a 20–6 record after joining the team in February 1980, helping Milwaukee to its first division title in four years. The Bucks would win the division in all five seasons that Lanier was with the club in the 1980s.

2. STEPHON MARBURY TO THE MINNESOTA TIMBERWOLVES FOR RAY ALLEN AND A FIRST-ROUND DRAFT PICK, 1996

It's hard to believe that Bucks general manager Mike Dunleavy was booed lustfully by the Bucks faithful at the Bradley Center on the night of the 1996 NBA draft. Most Bucks fans wanted the big name in Stephon Marbury and were livid when Dunleavy dealt the point guard to the Timberwolves. It didn't take long for Ray Allen to win the fans over. Allen owned the prettiest shot in Bucks history. As a three-point sharpshooter, he made up one-third of the "Big Three" and helped lead Milwaukee back to relevance at the turn of the century. The first-round pick was exchanged with Minnesota for big man Andrew Lang, who did not make an impact in Milwaukee, but most general managers would take Allen over Marbury straight up any day. Yes, Marbury's career scoring numbers may be better than Allen's, but Marbury spent the first eight years of his career with four different teams and was a detriment to every locker room he entered. Allen has proven himself to be a team guy and a winner.

1. FLYNN ROBINSON AND CHARLIE PAULK TO THE CINCINNATI ROYALS FOR OSCAR ROBERTSON, 1970

Oscar Robertson was the missing piece of the Bucks puzzle for winning an NBA championship. "The Big O" helped Milwaukee become the fastest expansion franchise to win a title by doing so in the team's third season. Robertson led Milwaukee back to the finals in 1974. Flynn Robinson was the better of the two players the Bucks sent to the Royals in the deal, and he averaged 13 points a game in his best season after getting traded. Charlie Paulk's best season came the year after the trade, as well, when he averaged nine points and four rebounds a game for Cincinnati. Robinson and Paulk were a small price to pay for a seasoned Hall of Fame point guard in Robertson.

WHAT'S THE WORST TRADE IN BUCKS HISTORY?

66 The Bucks have a tradition of making some questionable front office decisions. Passing over Milwaukee native Terry Porter for Jerry Reynolds in the 1985 draft was certainly a big one. Even though Milwaukee drafted Julius Erving in 1972, "Dr. J" never played for the Bucks, opting to stay in the ABA before being sold to Philadelphia in 1976. As for trades, Milwaukee came up on the losing end of a three-team trade, sending Mo Williams to Cleveland in return for Luke Ridnour and Damon Jones. Williams instantly became a first time All-Star for the Cavaliers and a perfect complement for LeBron James. As for the worst trade hall of shame? Here are three deals the Bucks wish they never made.

3. KAREEM ABDUL-JABBAR AND WALT WESLEY TO THE LOS ANGELES LAKERS FOR ELMORE SMITH, BRIAN WINTERS, DAVID MEYERS, JUNIOR BRIDGEMAN, AND FUTURE CONSIDERATIONS, 1975

The Kareem Abdul-Jabbar trade makes both the best and worst lists. This was and still is the biggest trade in

Bucks history. Admittedly, the Bucks had to get rid of Kareem—their hands were tied. Abdul-Jabbar wanted out of Milwaukee, and the team wanted to get something in return. The ABA was still around and desperate for a gate attraction so the Bucks were trapped—if they didn't deal Abdul-Jabbar, he would simply jump leagues, and Milwaukee would get nothing. Yes, they did get four players in return, including Brian Winters and Junior Bridgeman, but any trade where a team has to send away the NBA's all-time leading scorer has to be considered a questionable one. Abdul-Jabbar led the Bucks to their one title, but he led the Lakers to five championships in 14 seasons.

2. RAY ALLEN, KEVIN OLLIE, AND RON "FLIP" MURRAY TO THE SEATTLE SUPERSONICS FOR GARY PAYTON AND DESMOND MASON, 2003

This one was a shocker. Ray Allen was the face of the Bucks franchise, but George Karl and Ernie Grunfeld wanted to shake things up, so they made this five-player deal. What made this trade so awful was that Gary Payton could not get out of Milwaukee fast enough. He was in the final year of his contract and had zero intention of re-signing to stay with the Bucks. Payton played exactly 34 games for Milwaukee, including six in the playoffs, as he led the Bucks to a first-round exit against the Nets. Desmond Mason was a nice player, a hard worker, and a good team guy, but he was no Ray Allen. The deal allowed the Bucks to feature Michael Redd, but most general managers would take Allen over Redd any day. Allen made the All-Star team four times in Seattle and would finally win a championship ring with the Boston Celtics in 2008.

1. DIRK NOWITSKI AND PAT GARRITY TO THE DALLAS MAVERICKS FOR ROBERT "TRACTOR" TRAYLOR, 1998

Talk about a draft-day blunder. The Bucks had no intention of keeping Dirk Nowitski when they selected him with the ninth pick in the 1998 draft. Former Bucks head coach Don Nelson, then with Dallas, had wanted Nowitski badly, and he needed a team to make a deal with, so who better than his old team, the Bucks? Milwaukee selected Nowitski, and then Pat Garrity with the 19th pick, and packaged them to the Mavericks for Robert "Tractor" Traylor, who was taken sixth overall. Traylor was an overweight bust who lasted just two seasons in Milwaukee, averaging a mere 4.5 points per game. Nowitski, meanwhile, turned into an NBA MVP—the first European-born player to win the award—and was a cornerstone of those terrific Dallas teams of the 2000s. Plus, Garrity turned out to be a serviceable journeyman, lasting more than a decade in the NBA. Bob Weinhauer was the Bucks general manager who pulled off the Traylor blunder, and it's no wonder Weinhauer's run as Bucks GM lasted about as long as Traylor's stint in Milwaukee—another two years or so.

BACK TO SCHOOL—ON WISCONSIN, GO MARQUETTE

WHO'S THE BADGERS' BIGGEST RIVAL: IOWA OR MINNESOTA?

67 Which do Badgers hate more, Hawkeyes or Gophers? You'd think that in recent years, it would be Iowa. The Hawkeyes shattered the Badgers' Rose Bowl hopes in 2004. Then a year later, Iowa ruined Barry Alvarez's going-away party at Camp Randall, upsetting Wisconsin in the head coach's final home game. There's history between the two schools. Back in 1999, Ron Dayne broke the NCAA career rushing record against Iowa. Even further back, the Badgers snapped a 23-game winless streak when they played Iowa at Camp Randall in 1969. A decade earlier, Wisconsin humbled the defending Big 10–champion Hawkeyes 25–16. The victory set the tone for UW's first undisputed conference title in 47 years.

Players and coaches have switched sides. Barry Alvarez got his start in college coaching at Iowa, and when he was hired at UW, he took a handful of Iowa assistants with him. Bret Bielema played for Iowa—he even has a Hawkeye tattoo. And it's not just football. Sam Okey transferred from Wisconsin to play basketball at Iowa. Jason Bohannon grew up a short drive from Iowa City and yet chose to play hoops for Bo Ryan in Madison. There's no question that Iowa is a bitter rival of Wisconsin—but not the biggest. That title belongs to the Gophers of Minnesota.

Every autumn, the Badgers and Gophers battle for Paul Bunyan's Axe, the traveling trophy given to the winner of the border battle since 1948, but the football rivalry dates back much further than that. The two schools' first meeting on the gridiron was back in 1890, and it's the oldest and most-played rivalry in college football. You've heard of the often-overused phrase, "You can throw out the record books when those two teams meet." This is one rivalry where that cliché holds true, because no matter how good or how bad Minnesota or Wisconsin is, it's always a tough football game. The players love it, since most of them know each other. Both rosters are dominated by players from these two states that are separated by the Mississippi River.

The football games themselves usually add fuel to the fire. In 1993, the Gophers handed the Rose Bowl–bound Badgers their lone loss of the season, costing them a shot at a national championship. In 1999, Alvarez watched the game from his hospital room while awaiting knee surgery at the Mayo Clinic in Minnesota and saw his team pull off a gutsy win at the Metrodome that helped UW to its third Rose Bowl under Alvarez. In a 2005 game, the Badgers scored 10 points in the final 1:17, capped by a blocked punt with 30 seconds left, resulting in one of the most incredible victories in the Alvarez era. The rivalry is so highly regarded that Minnesota officials have made sure the team opens with Wisconsin in the first game at the Gophers' new outdoor football stadium in 2009. Iowa is now a "protected rival" of Wisconsin—because the Big Ten has 11 schools and plays only eight conference games, the schedule rotates, but every school protects two rivalries and Wisconsin's rivals are now Iowa *and* Minnesota.

In basketball, Dick Bennett scored one of his biggest home wins in 1997 when the Badgers upset a Gophers team in the final regular-season game before Minnesota went on to the Final Four. It was such an emotional win that the normally humble Bennett pumped his fists as he left the Field House floor. Hockey adds another dimension to the rivalry. It seems like Minnesota and Wisconsin play big game after big game on the ice every year. The two schools are the traditional powers of the WCHA and between them own 13 national championships. In 1981, UW knocked off Minnesota 6–3 to win the NCAA Tournament. That team was called "the Backdoor Badgers," since they barely made the tournament field. Most Badgers hockey players who've done it will tell you that there's nothing like winning the Final Five Tournament in the Twin Cities, especially if you have to beat the Gophers along the way.

Simply put, the Badgers and Hawkeyes are heated rivals. The Badgers and Gophers are hated rivals.

201

WHAT ARE THE TOP FIVE MOMENTS IN CAMP RANDALL HISTORY?

68 Camp Randall Stadium opened on November 3, 1917. It's the oldest stadium in the Big Ten Conference, the fourth-oldest in big-time college football, and one of the largest in seating capacity, at 80,321. Over the years, the Badgers have built Camp Randall into one of the toughest places to play in the country—truly, they gain a home-field advantage there. It's a stadium filled with classic moments in Wisconsin sports history. Here are the top five.

5. OCTOBER 11, 1969; WISCONSIN 23, IOWA 17

We must acknowledge that Camp Randall wasn't always the home of a winning football program. UW was known much more for its counterculture student body than its football team in the late 1960s. However, for at least one afternoon in October 1969, that all changed. Wisconsin snapped a 23-game winless streak by beating Iowa and giving Head Coach John Coatta his first win—in his third season! Badgers fans were so moved after snapping the nation's longest losing streak that they stormed the field and carried Coatta off it on their shoulders.

4. NOVEMBER 10, 1962: WISCONSIN 37, NORTHWESTERN 6

You don't normally think of both Wisconsin and Northwestern as national powers in the same season, but in 1962, that was certainly the case. The Badgers were ranked eighth in the country, and the Wildcats were the top-ranked club in the land. Behind quarterback Ron Vander Kelen and end Pat Richter, the Badgers turned a 10–0 halftime lead into a laugher by scoring 21 points in the first seven minutes of the third quarter. Wisconsin would win 37–6, helping UW jump from eighth to fourth in the national polls. The victory helped the team reach the Rose Bowl.

3. SEPTEMBER 12, 1981: WISCONSIN 21, MICHIGAN 14

From the time John F. Kennedy was president all the way until Ronald Reagan moved into the White House, you could always count on one thing: Wisconsin losing to Michigan in football. UW hadn't beaten the Wolverines since 1962, and Michigan came to Madison in 1981 riding high as the No. 1 team in the country. Plus, Michigan had outscored Wisconsin 176–0 in their previous four meetings. However, the Badgers played their best game of the season, and

Chucky Davis scored with two seconds left in the second quarter to give UW a seven-point lead. Wisconsin would take the lead for good in the third quarter, thanks to a John Williams 71-yard touchdown on a screen pass, and the rest is history. Although, only 68,733 (10,000 less than capacity at the time) bothered to show up to watch, those who did saw a game for the ages. It was the biggest home upset in school history.

2. OCTOBER 31, 1942: WISCONSIN 17, OHIO STATE 7

Halloween is a sacred holiday in Madison. Before the ghosts and goblins started the tradition of taking over State Street, another group of monsters haunted the No. 1 team in the country, Ohio State. Elroy "Crazylegs" Hirsch led a group of Badgers to the school's first victory over a top-ranked team in the country. Wisconsin took a 10–0 halftime lead and never looked back, beating the Buckeyes 17–7 in front of a then-record crowd of more than 45,000 at Camp Randall.

1. NOVEMBER 13, 1999: WISCONSIN 41, IOWA 3

This was as much a coronation as a football game. Ron Dayne passed Ricky Williams to become college foot-ball's all-time leading rusher, and in the process, helped Wisconsin clinch its second straight trip to the Rose Bowl and third under Barry Alvarez. "The Great Dayne" broke the record with just over four minutes left in the first half. The play was 23-zone. Dayne gained 31 yards and smashed the record. In all, Dayne rushed for 216 yards and a touchdown that day to give him 6,397 yards in his fantastic college career. Jay Wilson, a 25-year veteran covering sports in Madison—who at the time was the sports director at WKOW-TV—said of the atmosphere, "It was just so unique, to see the NCAA rushing record fall and Wisconsin clinch another trip to the Rose Bowl. It was the best atmosphere I've seen at Camp Randall."

WHAT ARE THE TOP FIVE INDIVIDUAL BOWL PERFORMANCES BY A BADGER?

69 It wasn't that long ago when simply qualifying for a bowl game would be reason enough to hit State Street. (But really, do you need a reason to hit State Street?) However, after Barry Alvarez's arrival, Wisconsin playing in a bowl game became almost as regular as the ball dropping on Times Square. The Wisconsin Badgers played in six bowl games in 101 years of football before Alvarez arrived in Madison in 1991. Alvarez led the team to 11 bowl games in his 16 seasons, finishing with an 8–3 bowl record at the time of his retirement.

Sure, you remember your favorite highlight of your favorite Badgers bowl game, don't you? Maybe it was Darrell Bevell weaving his way through UCLA defenders and somehow finding the end zone at the 1994 Rose Bowl. Or perhaps it was a play behind a play, like Jack Ikegwuonu running down Arkansas running back Darren McFadden at the 9-yard line, saving a touchdown (the Razorbacks would miss a field goal and come up empty on their opening drive) and setting the tone for a Wisconsin upset of Arkansas in the 2007 Capital One Bowl. Those are great individual moments, but which Badgers had the greatest bowl games in school history? Here are the top five.

5. BRIAN CALHOUN, 2006 CAPITAL ONE BOWL

Playing in his last game as a Badger, Brian Calhoun helped Barry Alvarez win the final game of his coaching career. Calhoun ran for 213 yards and a touchdown, and Wisconsin upset seventh-ranked Auburn 24–10. His lone touchdown was a 33-yard score to put the game away in the fourth quarter. Like the other individuals in the top five, Calhoun was named the game's Most Valuable Player.

4. BRENT MOSS, 1994 ROSE BOWL

Wisconsin's run for the roses was the feel-good story of the 1993 college football season. It was topped with a cherry in Pasadena. Brent Moss ran the ball 36 times for 158 yards and scored two touchdowns as Wisconsin knocked off UCLA 21–16 for UW's first New Year's Day bowl victory.

3. TERRELL FLETCHER, 1995 HALL OF FAME BOWL

Terrell Fletcher was forced to carry the load when Brent Moss was kicked off the team earlier in the season because

207

of a drug charge. Fletcher saved his best game for last and ran wild against Duke in Tampa. The future San Diego Charger rushed for 190 of his 241 yards in the second half. He also scored twice and set a school bowl record with 39 carries as Wisconsin beat Duke 34–20.

2. RON VANDER KELEN, 1963 ROSE BOWL

This Badgers quarterback almost pulled off the greatest comeback in college bowl history. Ron Vander Kelen rallied Wisconsin from a 42–14 deficit, thanks to three TD passes and a touchdown run. In all, Vander Kelen set Rose Bowl records with 48 passing attempts, 33 completions, and 401 yards. The 401 yards stood as a school record for 30 years. The only reason Vander Kelen is not No. 1 on this list is that the comeback fell short—second-ranked Wisconsin lost to No. 1 USC 42–37.

1. RON DAYNE, 1999 ROSE BOWL

"The Great Dayne" rushed for 200 or more yards in three of his four bowl games at Wisconsin. The 1999 Rose Bowl was his finest hour. Not many gave UW a chance against UCLA. In fact, CBS analyst Craig James said Wisconsin was "the worst team ever to play in a Rose Bowl." Dayne made James eat his words as he ran roughshod over the Bruins' defense for 246 yards on 27 carries—an average of over nine yards a carry. Dayne scored four touchdowns as the Badgers beat UCLA 38–31.

WHICH WAS THE BEST BADGERS FOOTBALL TEAM?

70 This argument is for modern-day UW football—any team since 1952 (the Badgers' first trip to the Rose Bowl). Wisconsin had three unbeaten seasons in 1901, 1906, and 1912, but back then, the Badgers beat teams like the Milwaukee Medicine, Hyde Park High School, Knox, and Lawrence—not your traditional college football powerhouses. Therefore, those teams just get an honorable mention here.

The first criterion: the best Wisconsin team had to win a Rose Bowl. Sorry, 1952, 1959, and 1963 Badgers. That leaves us with three clubs—1993, 1998, and 1999. The second criterion: the team could not lose to Cincinnati. That eliminates the 1999 team. The third criterion: the Badgers had to face the Big Ten's best teams. This is where the 1993 team edges the one from 1998.

Even though the 1998 team (11–1) had a better record than the 1993 team (10–1–1), the 1993 team had to face both Ohio State and Michigan; the 1998 team avoided playing the Buckeyes because of the Big Ten's unbalanced schedule. Yes, the 1993 team lost at Minnesota, but it was a crazy night in Minneapolis, and in a rivalry game anything can happen. There was nothing to be ashamed of in losing to the Gophers on the road. The tie in 1993 against Ohio State came one week after the biggest win of the season. Barry Alvarez and the Badgers finally beat Michigan the week before they played the Buckeyes. However, with the victory over the Wolverines came the adversity—the post-game incident known as "the Stampede."

Moments after beating Michigan, excited students rushed onto Camp Randall's turf, and in the process some of the students fell underneath the crush of their onrushing classmates. When joy turned to panic, members of the UW football team came to the rescue of their fellow students. Players pulled classmates off each other. One quick-thinking player, Michael Brin, performed CPR. In all, about 70 students suffered injuries, but thankfully, everyone survived. Barry Alvarez said years later that it was the biggest emotional roller coaster of any day of his career. His team had registered a breakthrough victory by beating Michigan, and minutes after the game had ended, his players were in tears, not knowing whether some of their classmates would survive the celebration.

One week later, Wisconsin refocused and tied Ohio State; it wasn't a win, but the tie helped end a 30-year Rose Bowl drought. The 1993 team was led by a sophomore quarterback wise beyond his years in Darrell Bevell, a dynamic duo in the backfield of Brent Moss and Terrell Fletcher, and a bend-but-don't break defense that did enough to win games. The 1993 offense still holds the school record for total offense, as it averaged 455 yards a game.

The 1998 team was certainly no slouch. The defense was probably better than the 1993 edition. There's no question that the best player on either team was Ron Dayne for the 1998 squad. But Bevell gets the edge at quarterback over Mike Samuel, and the offensive line in 1993 was a smidge better than the 1998 version. What pushes the 1993 team over the top is the intangible of doing something no other Wisconsin team had done before: winning a Rose Bowl. The 1993 team was a collection of pioneers, a group that was far greater than the sum of its parts. They were the first class truly recruited by Barry Alvarez, and along with the scholarship players, a collection of walk-ons began a tradition of contribution which continues today. They were a scrappy, hungry football team, and the players had a chip the size of Bascom Hill on their shoulders—after all, the seniors on the 1993 team were just three seasons removed from a 1–10 campaign. This group changed the football culture at Wisconsin since the team had won so little for so long before it. It had been nine years since the school's last winning season.

Both the 1993 team and the 1998 club capped their seasons with late defensive stands to hold off the UCLA Bruins and win the Rose Bowl. Both clubs finished ranked sixth in the final Associated Press poll and fifth in the final

USA Today Coaches' Poll. The 1998 team was labeled "the worst team ever to play in a Rose Bowl" before the game by CBS analyst Craig James. Obviously, that proved to be false. But, the 1998 team was the second-best team to represent Wisconsin in the Rose Bowl, just behind the 1993 team, which gets the edge for trailblazing a path to Pasadena.

WHO'S THE BETTER RUNNING BACK, DAYNE OR AMECHE?

71 Who was better, "the Great Dayne" or "the Horse"? Ron Dayne and Alan Ameche were two terrific running backs and two Heisman Trophy winners—the only two Badgers to win college football's top honor. There are similarities between the two men. Ameche played fullback. Dayne played tailback like a fullback. Both won the Heisman in their senior seasons. Both left college as the NCAA career rushing leader. But suppose you are coaching the Badgers in the Rose Bowl. Who carries the load?

AMECHE

Remember that famous story about Michael Jordan getting cut from his high school basketball team? Alan Ameche didn't even touch the ball in his first college football game—a JV game, at that! However, it took less than a month for Ameche to work his way into the starting lineup, and the Kenosha native made the most of his opportunity. Listed at 205 pounds, "the Horse" was ahead of his time. He was the heaviest player on the Badgers offense and the only starter over 200 pounds, yet Ameche rushed for 3,345 yards (then the NCAA record) and 25 touchdowns in his four seasons in Madison. He rushed for more than 100 yards 16 times and led the Badgers to their first postseason appearance, the 1953 Rose Bowl. What's even more amazing is that thanks to an NCAA rule requiring players to play both ways, Ameche was forced to play defense during his final two seasons and started at middle linebacker.

DAYNE

At 252 pounds, Ron Dayne in the open field was more like a runaway train than a Great Dane. The plan was to ease the Berlin, New Jersey, native into the running attack early on in his career. However, after running for the first of his 33 100-yard games, against Penn State in the fourth week of his freshman season, there was no slowing down "the Great Dayne." He rushed for at least 200 yards 14 times in his four years at UW, and his 339-yard performance against Hawaii in 1996 is still a Badgers record. Dayne finished college with the NCAA record of 7,125 yards and 71 touchdowns.

THE VERDICT

Barry Alvarez once said he'd never seen a more dominant running back than Ron Dayne, and there was no stopping big number 33 when he got "lathered up." Dayne helped

Wisconsin become the first Big Ten team to win back-to-back Rose Bowls and ran for 200 yards in both wins in Pasadena. He was a running back in a linebacker's body who could run over defensive tackles and sprint past defensive backs. Ameche was good. Dayne was the best.

WHO'S THE BEST BADGER WIDE RECEIVER?

72 Most Badgers fans know Pat Richter as the former UW Athletic Director. He was the man who hired Barry Alvarez. He was the man who took over an athletic department more than $2 million in debt and turned it into the businesslike model that turned the deficit into a multimillion-dollar surplus. However, not all Badgers fans realize what a special football player Richter was in his day.

At 6'5", Richter was a huge target who could run. As a junior, he led the nation with 47 catches and eight touchdowns. He was a two-time All-American in 1961 and 1962, when he led the Big Ten in receptions both years. And Richter could do more than just catch passes. He could also punt—Richter led the conference in punting during his senior season. His finest hour came in his final game, the 1963 Rose Bowl. Richter caught 11 passes against top-ranked USC—a record that stood for 31 years.

The wide receiver position at UW could be the most underrated of all. There's been no shortage of outstanding wide receivers at Wisconsin. Al Toon, Donald Hayes, Chris

Chambers, Lee Evans, and Brandon Williams all excelled at Madison, and all went on to enjoy careers in the NFL. Pat Richter would also play on Sundays. He was a first-round draft pick for the Redskins and spent eight seasons in Washington.

You could make the case that Lee Evans was the best receiver in Badgers history. The numbers certainly support it. Evans is first and second in the UW record books for most receiving yards in a season and most receptions in a season. Evans also owns the school record for touch-downs in a season, with 13 in 2003. However, those are just numbers. Houston's David Klingler was once the college football record-holder for TD passes in a season. Do you consider Klingler the best quarterback in college football history? Not a chance. Evans is no David Klingler, but the point is that numbers are just that—numbers.

Richter was tough. He once played with a broken hand against Iowa in his senior season. The pain was so bad that Richter could only catch passes with his fingertips. That afternoon was one of his proudest as a player, as he helped the Badgers rout Iowa 42–14.

Richter bridged eras in college football. He was an all-around athlete at Madison East before enrolling at Madison in 1960. Richter was the final UW athlete to earn nine varsity letters in football, basketball, and baseball—and this was when freshman athletes were not eligible to participate at the varsity level. Richter was an innovator—

one of the first to utilize hand signals with his quarterback, Ron Vander Kelen. He finished his collegiate career with 121 catches for 1,873 yards and 15 touchdowns. Those numbers may not be eye-popping by today's standards, but in the early 1960s they were exceptional. Guys like Toon and Chambers were dominant in shorter stretches, but they were not as consistent as Richter was in the early 1960s. Richter is the only Badgers receiver and one of three Wisconsin players inducted into the College Football Hall of Fame. Pat Richter is the best wide receiver in UW football history.

WHO'S THE BEST BADGER QUARTERBACK?

73 Who's the best Badger quarterback: Darrell Bevell or Ron Vander Kelen? Both led Wisconsin to the Rose Bowl. One won, one lost. One rewrote the UW passing records, while the other basically did his damage in one season. Bevell and Vander Kelen are the two top quarterbacks in Wisconsin history—but which one is the best?

The quarterback position at Wisconsin is almost like an umpire in baseball. When he's good, you don't really notice him. When he's bad, everybody knows it. In the Alvarez era and beyond, the Badgers quarterback has been more of a game manager, a guy who is tough, hard-nosed, and willing to run the ball if need be. Guys like Mike Samuel, Jim Sorgi, Brooks Bollinger, and John Stocco were all serviceable, solid college quarterbacks, but it was Darrell Bevell who set the mold.

Bevell enrolled at UW as a 22-year-old freshman. He began his collegiate career at Northern Arizona and redshirted his freshman year under Offensive Coordinator Brad Childress. Bevell then left on a Mormon mission in

1990, before reuniting with Childress in Madison in the fall of 1992. Bevell took over for Jay Macias midway through the 1992 season and led the Badgers to their first Rose Bowl in three decades in 1993. Bevell's 21-yard touchdown run to help beat UCLA for UW's first Rose Bowl win ever is one of the greatest single plays, if not *the* greatest single play, in Badgers football history. Bevell left Wisconsin as the school's all-time leader in passing yards (7,686), attempts (1,052), completions (646), and touchdown passes (59).

Bevell's Badgers were the first squad from Madison to play in Pasadena since Ron Vander Kelen's team did so in 1963. It's a wonder that Vander Kelen was even in college, let alone playing for UW, during that historic Rose Bowl. The Green Bay native actually went to the Rose Bowl as a reserve during his sophomore season, but after hurting his knee the following year, Vander Kelen wound up dropping out of school in 1961 because of eligibility issues. He spent the year working in construction, although he never gave up on his dream to start for the Badgers. In 1962, his wish came true after he had his final year of eligibility restored. Vander Kelen threw for 14 touchdowns and 1,562 yards during the 1962 season. He led Wisconsin to an 8–1 regular-season record, a Big Ten title, the No. 2 ranking in the country, and a trip to the Rose Bowl. The high point of the regular season came on November 10, 1962, when the Badgers crushed then–No. 1 Northwestern 37–6 in one of the biggest wins in Camp Randall Stadium history.

Vander Kelen's legend grew in Pasadena in one of the greatest college football bowl games of all time. The right-handed senior threw for 401 yards and nearly erased a 42–14 fourth-quarter deficit, only to come up just shy as Wisconsin lost to USC 42–37. Vander Kelen was named the game's MVP in the loss. USC was the top-ranked team in the country that year and held on to win the national championship.

Bevell won the Rose Bowl. Vander Kelen did not. However, USC was the best team in college football against Vander Kelen, while UCLA was ranked 13th against Bevell. Vander Kelen proved himself to be a playmaker and a difference-maker in his one year as a starter. Bevell did his best with his abilities, but he was more of a game manager. Bevell's pinnacle came in the Rose Bowl win as a sophomore. When he was a senior in 1995, UW struggled to 4–5–2 mark. The two quarterbacks rank the first and second in school history for most passing yards in a game. Bevell set the record with 423 yards against Minnesota in 1993, breaking Vander Kelen's mark of 401 in the 1963 Rose Bowl. Both games were losses. But Vander Kelen had more good days than bad during the 1962 season, losing just two games as a starter. It's close, but the nod goes to Vander Kelen as the Badgers' best quarterback for his magical season in 1962, capped by one of the greatest bowl performances in college football history.

WHO'S THE BEST BADGER OFFENSIVE LINEMAN?

74 If Wisconsin does one thing well year in and year out, it's run the football. There's a reason why UW has turned into the modern-day "Tailback U." Brent Moss, Terrell Fletcher, Ron Dayne, Michael Bennett, Anthony Davis, Brian Calhoun, and P. J. Hill all ran wild for one reason—a dominant Badgers offensive line.

From Joe Panos to Cory Raymer to Chris McIntosh to Aaron Gibson, the Badgers were never short of beef up front. The foundation of the Alvarez era was set up by a huge offensive line. But even before Alvarez, the Badgers were blessed with some top-of-the-line talent, like Dennis Lick in the mid-1970s and Paul Gruber in the mid-1980s. However, when searching for the best of the best, there's only one—Joe Thomas.

You don't usually think of offensive linemen as athletes. You think of them as "hogs" or "the big uglies," but not athletes. That's why Thomas was so unique. He was a 300-pound guy who could run like a fullback and had feet like a tight end. In fact, he began his career in Madison as a true freshman playing tight end, as well as defensive end. In high school, Thomas was one of the better punters in Wisconsin, coming out of Brookfield Central High School, not to mention a state shot-put champion.

Even after he found his calling as a tackle on the Badgers offensive line, Thomas found other ways to contribute. When Wisconsin was decimated with injuries to its defensive line during his junior season in 2005, Thomas volunteered to play both offense and defense against Auburn in the Capitol One Bowl. But when he was playing defense, Thomas suffered a torn ACL, which required knee surgery. The level-headed Thomas was such a team-first guy that he refused to dwell on his injury on the field after the game. He simply wanted to enjoy another Badgers win—a major upset of Auburn in Barry Alvarez's final game as UW head coach.

The setback was a blessing in disguise for all parties, since Thomas decided against entering the NFL draft in order to return to Madison for his senior season. It was a good decision, to say the least. Thomas became the first Badger to win the Outland Trophy in 2006, finishing his career with a victory over Darren McFadden, Felix Jones, and Arkansas in the Capitol One Bowl.

Thomas started 39 games in his career in Madison and gave up just six sacks. He was drafted third overall by the Cleveland Browns in the 2007 NFL draft. It was the earliest that a Badgers lineman had ever been selected. But in typical, low-key Thomas style, he passed up the opportunity to participate in draft-day festivities in New York City with the other top-10 picks. Instead, "the Regular Joe" spent the morning fishing on Lake Michigan with his father. Yes, he was thrilled to get drafted that high, but Thomas said he wanted to spend the day with his dad doing what they loved.

Thomas excelled in the classroom, as well. He graduated with a 3.5 GPA and won the Big Ten Medal of Honor in 2007, given annually to a scholar-athlete from each conference school. Thomas also won an $18,000 postgraduate scholarship for being a National Scholarship Athlete.

Thomas is a big-picture guy. The week before the 2007 draft, he said that not only did he want to become a Pro Bowl offensive tackle, his goal was to have his bust in Canton, Ohio. Thomas made it to the Pro Bowl in each of his first two seasons with the Browns, but only time will tell if he will someday become the third UW player to be inducted into the Pro Football Hall of Fame.

WHO'S THE BEST BADGER DEFENSIVE BACK?

75 The cupboard was almost bare for Barry Alvarez upon his arrival in Madison in 1991. The one diamond in the rough was Troy Vincent. He was the best athlete on Alvarez's first UW squad and his first All-American. Vincent was a lockdown cornerback who would have posted better interception numbers if opposing quarterbacks had thrown his way more often. Even on a team that won just one game in 1991, Vincent was still named the Big Ten's Co-Defensive Player of the Year. He also made an impact returning punts—he ranks third on UW's all-time list for punt-return yardage.

Jamar Fletcher was also a game-breaker and a difference-maker. In 2000, he became the only UW player to win the prestigious Jim Thorpe Award given to the nation's top defensive back. Fletcher was also the Big Ten's Defensive Player of the Year in 2000, and he left Madison as the school's all-time leader in interceptions with 21.

Two great cornerbacks—both were All-Americans, and both were first-round draft picks by the Miami Dolphins.

Vincent turned out to be the better pro, but Fletcher was better at the collegiate level. Fletcher was tested almost weekly, and he passed every test. Vincent was avoided, while Fletcher was challenged. More times than not, Fletcher stepped up to the challenge and made the opposition pay in the form of an interception returned for a touchdown. Five times in his three seasons, he picked off a pass and scored a Badgers touchdown, including one against Cade McNown in the 1999 Rose Bowl. Fletcher was also the guy who helped spark the "Jump Around" tradition. It was his 52-yard interception return for a touchdown late in the third quarter against Purdue's Drew Brees that not only turned the game around for Wisconsin on that memorable October night in 1998, but also led to the introduction of "Jump Around." If LeRoy Butler invented the "Lambeau Leap," then Jamar Fletcher invented "Jump Around."

In all, Fletcher returned his 21 picks for 459 yards—almost double the yardage of the next-closest Badger (Neovia Greyer, 285). He was simply the best athlete on the turf every time he set foot on the field.

If this was a discussion of who was the better pro cornerback, there would be no discussion—it would be Troy Vincent. After all, Vincent was a five-time Pro Bowler. Fletcher never reached those heights in the NFL, bouncing from the Dolphins to the Chargers and then the Lions, but in college football, Fletcher was UW's best defensive back.

WHICH WAS THE BEST BADGERS HOCKEY TEAM?

76 For the uninitiated, the Badgers hockey team is the most underrated sports entity outside of the city of Madison, but it has been one of the constants on campus. The team is competitive year in and year out, and the game-day experience is unlike any others. There are chants and cheers led by the student section and the Badgers band. When Wisconsin scores, the opposing goaltender hears about it: "Sieve! Sieve! Sieve!" It's one of the great, wholesome heckles in college sports. And oh by they way, the Badgers also have a terrific hockey product on the ice. They've won six national championships under three different coaches, including the legendary late "Badger Bob" Johnson, Jeff Sauer, and current coach and former player Mike Eaves. Wisconsin has won a national title in hockey in each of the last four decades—but which team stands above the rest?

Some might point to the most recent national championship team of 2005–2006. The team did win 30 games, including the first hockey game played at Lambeau Field in Green Bay, defeating Ohio State 4–2 in the "Tundra

Classic" in front of 40,000 fans. However, that team finished second in the WCHA and lost in their conference tournament. It also enjoyed a home-ice advantage in the NCAA Tournament, playing in the Frozen Four at the Bradley Center in Milwaukee.

There are only two teams in Wisconsin history to win the trifecta of college hockey: the regular-season title, the conference playoff crown, and the national championship. The 1989–1990 team was the last squad to pull off that hat trick, going 36–9–1. The 36 wins rank second in UW history—one shy of the school record set 13 years earlier by the other team to pull off the trifecta, the 1976–1977 squad. It's that team which is the greatest ever to wear the cardinal and white.

The 1976–1977 team won a school-record 37 games and lost just seven, with one tie. "Badger Bob" Johnson led the team to a league title with a 26–5–1 WCHA record in the regular season. The team never lost two games in a row, and down the stretch it went an amazing 22–1–1.

That was a star-studded team. Current head coach Mike Eaves was one of the captains and an All-American. The coach's son, Mark Johnson, was a high-scoring rookie and another All-American. Johnson's future Olympic teammate, Bob Suter, was on the team, along with All-American Craig Norwich and John Taft, who anchored the Badgers defense. Goaltender Julian Baretta was an

All-American and was named the NCAA Tournament's Most Valuable Player.

Even with the accolades, the Badgers still needed a clutch overtime goal from Steve Alley to beat Michigan in the championship game 6–5. It was a fitting end, since the Wolverines beat Wisconsin in Madison in the season opener for one of Bucky's seven losses that season. Alley's goal 23 seconds into overtime was a perfect way to end a near-perfect season for the best Wisconsin hockey team of all-time, the 1976–1977 club.

THE STATE'S COLLEGIATE ALL-TIME STARTING TEAM

77 POINT GUARD

The state of Wisconsin isn't considered a national hotbed for basketball talent, but maybe it should be. There's certainly an impressive list of those who have played college basketball in the state. The All-Time team starting five could stack up against any in the country. Here's Wisconsin's fabulous five of college basketball, starting with the point guard.

This is probably the toughest of the five positions to determine, simply because there are so many options. How deep is the state's history at point guard? Marquette's Butch Lee was an All-American and the 1977 NCAA Tournament's Most Outstanding Player, leading the Warriors to the national title, but Lee only receives an honorable mention. Apologies go out to Doc Rivers and Travis Diener, also of Marquette, and sorry to UW–Green Bay legend Tony Bennett. The Badgers also had a couple of standout point guards in lockdown defender Mike Kelley and Rick Olson, who could score at will. All were terrific college players who had areas of expertise: Diener and Bennett were sharpshooters, Kelley was a defensive specialist, Al McGuire called Lee a "silent assassin" because he was such a competitor, and Rivers could score from anywhere on the floor, including half-court, which he did to upset fifth-ranked Notre Dame in 1981. But the guy who could do it all was Devin Harris, the best point guard in state history.

The 6'3", 175-pound guard out of Wauwatosa East High School became the first Badger to be named the Big Ten's Most Valuable Player in 54 years in 2003–2004. That same year, Harris was the Big Ten Tournament's Most Outstanding Player. Harris was lightning-quick and could create his own shot from anywhere on the floor. He averaged 15 points a game in his three-year career, including 19.5 points per game in his junior season. Harris was clutch, as well. In March 2003, he hit the game-winning free throw with 0.4 seconds remaining against Illinois to clinch back-to-back Big Ten titles and UW's first outright conference championship in 56 years. He was also an above-average defender who could keep up with any opposing guard. On offense, Harris could use his speed to get past defenders, and if they doubled him, he could spot his open teammate. The most impressive statistic was that Harris rarely turned the ball over. In his career at UW, Harris averaged one turnover for every 20 minutes of action (3,356 minutes played, 170 turnovers). The Badgers won two conference championships in his three seasons in Madison and made it past the first round of the NCAA Tournament each year. In 2003, Harris led Wisconsin to the Sweet 16 in his sophomore season, when the Badgers lost to top-seeded Kentucky before the Wildcats were upset by Marquette. Harris left UW after his junior year and was drafted fifth overall in the 2004 NBA draft—the second-highest draft pick in school history. After helping the Dallas Mavericks to the NBA Finals in 2006, Harris now plays for the New Jersey Nets, where he continues to prove that they can ball in his home state of Wisconsin.

78 SHOOTING GUARD

This is a slam dunk, a no-doubter—the best shooting guard in state history is Dwayne Wade. Steve "the Homer" True, longtime radio voice of the Golden Eagles, was asked to name his starting five in state history, and he replied, "How about D. Wade and four other guys?"

The player who comes closest to Wade is another Marquette Golden Eagle, Jerel McNeal. Also from Chicago, McNeal left Marquette as the school's all-time leading scorer, breaking George Thompson's record set 40 years earlier. McNeal actually started as a defensive specialist, winning the Big East Defensive Player of the Year Award when he was a sophomore. In addition to the scoring record, McNeal is the Golden Eagles' all-time leader in steals. The greatest compliment one can give McNeal is that occasionally, his game reminds one of Dwyane Wade's.

Wade's finest moment at Marquette came in the 2003 NCAA Tournament, when he registered a triple-double in one of the biggest games of his college career, the Regional Finals. Wade scored 29 points, dished out 11 assists, grabbed 11 rebounds, and blocked four shots as the Golden Eagles upset top-seeded Kentucky 83–69 to punch a ticket to the Final Four. It was one of the greatest college basketball performances on one of the biggest stages. Wade did it all on that last Saturday of March 2003 in the Metrodome in Minneapolis. He scored. He passed. He rebounded. In the end, he rewarded Tom Crean for sticking with him, even though Wade had been academically ineligible his freshman year. Even when he couldn't play in games as a freshman, everyone heard the whispers: "Just wait until Dwyane Wade is allowed to play." Wade did not disappoint as he helped Marquette to its first Final Four in 26 years. In 2002–2003 Wade set a school record with 710 points in a single season. He's the best college basketball player in state history for his versatility and his ability to create his own shot. He's an incredible athlete who could jump out of the gym and took his defense seriously. After leaving Marquette at the end of his junior year, Wade went on to star on a bigger stage. He won an NBA championship with the Miami Heat, was named *Sports*

Illustrated's Sportsman of the Year in 2006, and won an Olympic gold medal—all before the age of 27.

79 CENTER

For a state that prides itself on big men, it's a bit odd that the big-man position has very few candidates. It really comes down to two players—Marquette's Jim Chones and Wisconsin's Rashard Griffith. Both players spent two seasons with their respective schools. Chones actually played less than two seasons, since he declared himself eligible for the ABA draft during his second season at Marquette. He was a first-round pick for the New York Knicks in 1972.

The two-season span gives us an easy way to compare the two big men. Chones averaged 19 points a game in his two years at Marquette, while Griffith averaged 15.5 during his two seasons at UW. Chones also gets the edge in rebounding—his average was 11.7, while Griffith's was nine. Chones was an All-American in 1972, but Griffith only made All-Conference in his sophomore season. The tipping point for Chones is winning games. Marquette went 49–1 during his time in Milwaukee, and when he declared for the draft, the Warriors were ranked second in the country. Griffith's Badgers were merely 31–25 in his two seasons in Madison and failed to make the postseason during his sophomore year, finishing 13–14. Chones spent 10 years in the ABA and NBA, winning a championship with the Los Angeles Lakers in 1980. Griffith was a second-round pick by the Bucks in 1995 but was content to play professionally in Europe. Of course, this argument is about college performance—Jim Chones outperformed Rashard Griffith and is the best center in state history.

80 SMALL FORWARD

Marquette's Steve Novak is the best pure shooter in state history. George Thompson, also of Marquette, is one of the great scorers to play college basketball in the state. But any argument about the best small forward in Wisconsin history boils down to two Badgers—Alando Tucker and Michael Finley.

Tucker had tremendous athleticism. He was a creator, always able to find his shot from just about anywhere on the floor. In 2006, Tucker was the first Badger to lead the Big Ten in conference-game scoring in 36 years. He was also just the third UW player to be named as a consensus first-team All-American. Tucker left Wisconsin as the school's all-time leader in points, field goals, free throws, free-throw attempts, and offensive rebounds. However, Tucker also ranks first in games played, games started, and minutes played, and that is what statistically separates Michael Finley from Alando Tucker.

Tucker owns all the Badgers records because of opportunity—he played in 19 more games than Finley, and yet the career scoring differential is merely 70 points.

This is not to belittle Alando Tucker in any way—he was a special talent. But Finley was more consistent and more versatile, which is why he is the greatest small forward in state history.

Finley is the only Badger to score 500 or more points and average more than 20 points per game in three separate seasons. Tucker never averaged 20 points a game for a full year. Finley was a bigger threat to the opposition for a longer period during his career than Tucker, and he had a better outside shot than Tucker, who was more of a "slashing" type of offensive threat. Finley could drive to the basket, as well, as evidenced by his monster dunks during his career, but those drives were possible because opposing players had to defend Finley's outside shot more than Tucker's. Finley also played on UW teams with little depth and was a marked man throughout his career. After Tracy Webster and Rashard Griffith, there were few threats on the Badgers clubs of the Finley era. Anyone who watched Finley drop 36 points on Missouri in the second round of the 1994 NCAA Tournament in Ogden, Utah, can attest to the fact that he had a target on his back at all times but still managed to score at will. Finley could do it all, which is why he edges Tucker as the state's best collegiate small forward.

POWER FORWARD

Marquette's Maurice Lucas was everything you could want in a power forward. He was tough, talented, and intimidating. Lucas played just 60 games for the Warriors in his two-year collegiate career but made the most of it, averaging a double-double each season. He averaged 15.7 points and 10.7 rebounds a game for Marquette—outstanding numbers when you consider all of the weapons Al McGuire had from 1972 to 1974. Lucas led the Warriors to the NCAA Championship Game in his sophomore season and led MU in scoring and rebounding for the game (21 points, 13 boards), but it wasn't enough to beat David Thompson and North Carolina State. Lucas was the only MU player to make the All-Tournament team that year, joining Thompson and UCLA great Bill Walton, among others. Marquette went 51–9 in Lucas's two seasons there, including a 28–2 mark at the MECCA.

The Badgers' best power forwards to offer in this argument are Danny Jones and Mike Wilkinson. Jones was a good scorer on bad teams. He ranks third on UW's all-time scoring list and finished his career with a 15.7 scoring average, but his teams failed to make the NCAA Tournament. Wilkinson's clubs had more success, winning over 75 percent of their games during his final three seasons, and he led his team to the Elite Eight in his senior year of 2005. He was a first-team All–Big Ten player his senior season and ranks seventh on the Badgers' all-time scoring list and third on the Badgers' all-time offensive rebounding and blocked shots lists.

Wilkinson and Jones were great players but not the best. Maurice Lucas stands above them all. He was a force under the boards who was also a consistent scoring option underneath. Lucas is the best power forward to play college hoops in Wisconsin, no question.

82 COACH

This fabulous five needs a man to guide them—someone who can push the right buttons to get the best out each individual; someone who knows the game inside and out, who can be one part recruiter to reel in talent and one part showman to make Wisconsin folk care about something other than football. That man is Al McGuire.

McGuire won 79 percent of his games at Marquette and is the school's all-time leader in wins. During his 13 seasons as the Warriors' head coach, he won 295 games and lost just 80. He made it to the Final Four twice: in 1974, falling to N.C. State in the title game, and in 1977, when he won the school's one and only national championship in his final game on the bench with tears streaming down his face. McGuire was so overcome with emotion that he couldn't hold back. That was Al McGuire, a man who knew a moment when he saw one. He was also a shrewd recruiter, often saying he knew a kid could play if his front yard was made of concrete. He was a showman—he knew he'd done his job if the cheap seats in the corner of the old MECCA were filled. McGuire was the guy who introduced into basketball's lexicon the terms *cupcake*, for a weak opponent, and *aircraft carrier*, for a wide-bodied big man.

As great a coach as he is, McGuire's going to need some assistants. Logic says to choose Harold "Bud" Foster, the only other man in state history to win an NCAA Division I championship, doing so with Wisconsin in 1941. Foster could teach old-school fundamentals.

Joining Foster on McGuire's bench would be Bo Ryan, the only coach to win four national titles in state history (four NCAA Division III titles with UW–Plattville). Dick Bennett could coach defense. Tom Crean could teach intensity. Bruce Pearl could be the recruiting coordinator. Crean and Bennett led teams to the Final Four, while Pearl made a magical run to the Sweet 16 with UWM in 2005 and has proven he can coach with the best of them. Can you imagine the coaching meetings with that group? It would be a small victory to be heard above the chatter. We have been spoiled in the state with these men—truly one terrific six-pack of coaches.

THE 2000 WISCONSIN BADGERS VERSUS THE 2003 MARQUETTE GOLDEN EAGLES: WHO WINS?

83 It's the best college basketball rivalry in the state—Wisconsin versus Marquette. They play every year, alternating sites, and it's the biggest non-conference game of the season for both teams. You can credit Al McGuire for taking the rivalry to another level. Back in 1974, the then-Warriors stunned Wisconsin with a last-second shot to win the game. McGuire jumped up on the scorer's table, and the MU coach pumped his fist right in front of a group of Badgers fans. One of those fans, Glenn Hughes, just happened to be the father of two of UW's stars, Kerry and Kim Hughes. In photographs of the infamous moment, Glenn can clearly be seen giving McGuire the single-digit salute.

Both schools have won one national title—Marquette under McGuire in 1977 and Wisconsin back in 1941. More recently, both schools made improbable runs to the Final

Four—UW in 2000 and MU in 2003. So what if those two most recent Final Four teams played one another? Which coach would be on the table jumping then?

The 2000 Badgers won four of their final six games just to sneak into the NCAA Tournament. They pulled off stunning upsets on their way to the Final Four—the most surprising coming against top-seeded Arizona in the second round. That team of Wildcats consisted of future NBA players Richard Jefferson, Luke Walton, Gilbert Arenas, Loren Woods, Michael Wright, and Jason Gardner. The tournament run even surprised UW point guard Mike Kelley, who said his friends laughed at him for picking Wisconsin to go as far as the Elite Eight in his own tournament bracket. Kelley even had UW losing in Regional Final, but he and the Badgers overachieved, helping Coach Dick Bennett to his only appearance in the Final Four.

Marquette was more of a known quantity heading into the 2003 NCAA Tournament. The Golden Eagles won the Conference USA regular-season title but struggled to beat Holy Cross in the first round. After knocking off Missouri in overtime, the Golden Eagles hit their stride in the Sweet 16. They beat Pittsburgh and stunned top-seeded Kentucky. Dwyane Wade was amazing en route to a triple-double in the regional final. Kentucky coach Tubby Smith said after the game, "We didn't have an answer for Wade." KU didn't have an answer for Marquette's Robert Jackson, either. The big man who had transferred back home to Milwaukee after starting his collegiate career at Mississippi State was insulted the day before by Kentucky's Marquis Estill, who said he didn't remember Jackson during his days in the SEC. Jackson made a lasting impression, scoring 24 points and pulling down 15 rebounds as Marquette earned its first trip to the Final Four in 26 years.

THE VERDICT

Big games are all about matchups. In this dream game, the key matchup is Wisconsin's Mike Kelley versus Marquette's Dwyane Wade. Even though Kelley stands just 6'3", he regularly had to guard the opposition's best player no matter what position he played. For example, Kelley once shut down future NBA standout Lamar Odom of Rhode Island, even though Odom was 7 inches taller than Kelley. Odom was held to just 10 points in a Badgers victory. Kelley left UW as the school's all-time steals leader but would have had his hands full guarding Dwyane Wade.

This dream game is played at the old MECCA in Milwaukee. The two-toned floor hosts this battle of Final Four titans. Even though Milwaukee is home to Marquette, the crowd is split 50–50—half red and white, the other half blue and gold. Both bands are playing at full volume, and since this is a nighttime tip-off, the sellout crowd has had all day to prepare, and they are ready to roll.

In this dream game, Wade gets off to a slow start, choosing to involve his teammates rather than to force things offensively. Wade is good at taking what the defense gives him, but Kelley is not giving up much early. Travis Diener's matchup with Jon Bryant turns out to be a shooting clinic, with each player hitting three first-half three-pointers. Steve Novak's two long-range threes are countered by Mark Vershaw's inside scoring. In another terrific matchup inside, Robert Jackson and Andy Kowske go toe to toe, banging each other as the refs let the two teams slug it out. After 20 minutes, it's tied at 28.

Early in the second half, it's obvious that the Badgers game plan is to get Roy Boone and Maurice Linton more involved offensively. However, the plan backfires. The Marquette players up their intensity and prove they can play defense, too. Their defense leads to offense. Wade, who was held to just four points in the first half, explodes, coming up with four steals, and he scores 14 points, including three thunderous dunks in the final 10 minutes.

Playing from behind is not UW's forte, and once the Marquette players build an eight-point lead, they never give it up. In the end, it's too much Dwyane Wade. He's just too talented and too athletic, and he proves to be the difference. Wade scores 18 points, grabs 11 rebounds, and dishes out six assists to go with four steals. Marquette beats Wisconsin 62–58 in this dream game between Final Four powers.

OUTSIDE THE
LINES

BETTER TRADITION: "JUMP AROUND" OR THE SAUSAGE RACE?

84 For the uninitiated, this is a puzzling question. Jumping around is something you do at any sporting event if your team does well. However, there's a specific meaning to the words *jump around* in Madison. It all began on Homecoming Night, October 10, 1999, against Purdue. Jamar Fletcher had just intercepted a Drew Brees pass and returned it for a Wisconsin touchdown, which happened to be the final play of the third quarter. The sellout crowd went nuts—almost 80,000 fans were on their feet, waiting through the TV timeout between the third and fourth quarters. Kevin Kluender of the UW marketing department was in charge of selecting what songs would play on the loudspeaker during breaks. Kluender wanted desperately to keep the crowd into the game. "We did our student race [on the scoreboard] as usual," Kluender recalled. "I just happened to see the song 'Jump Around' by House of Pain in there, I hit the button, I looked at the crowd, and it looked like popcorn. All the students were jumping."

It's really an incredible thing to watch a human popcorn popper, especially in the student sections in the northeast corner of the "Camp." Anyone who's covered a Badgers game gets a little uneasy during "Jump Around," since the press box literally shakes during the song, and the TVs sway as they hang from the ceiling. You can always tell a first-time reporter in the Camp Randall press box just by looking for frightened expressions between the third and fourth quarters. "Around college football these days, I think the stadium is known as much for that," says UW Director of Communications Justin Doherty. "It's a great visual."

The Badgers players agree. "When I am on the field, I get myself a few jumps in," says former UW running back P. J. Hill. "It gets the fans pumped up. It also gets my teammates pumped up."

"Jump Around" is not really a cheer—it's more of a seventh-inning stretch for college football. At Miller Park, the sausage race is something like a sixth-inning stretch for Brewers games. Like the tradition in Madison, the sausage race developed as a fluke.

In the early 1990s, the Brewers held animated sausage races on the scoreboard at County Stadium. They were such a hit with fans that the Klement's racing sausages were brought to life. Originally, the sausages would race live only on Sundays, and there were only three sausages during those early races: the Bratwurst, the Polish, and the Italian. The Hot Dog was added in the late 1990s. By the year 2000, the races were so popular that they became a staple at every home game. In 2006, the Brewers introduced a fifth sausage, the Chorizo.

The sausages are popular with ballplayers, as well. Mark Grace, Geoff Jenkins, and Hideo Nomo have all raced in the sausage suits. But not all players love the sausages. In July 2003, Pittsburgh Pirate Randall Simon took a swing and connected with the Italian sausage as it raced passed the visitors' dugout on the third-base side of the field. Mandy Block, a college student working for the Brewers, was inside the Italian sausage costume. She fell to the ground but was not hurt. Simon, however, instantly became Public Enemy No. 1 in Milwaukee. He was booed for the rest of his career when visiting Miller Park, even after changing teams. The incident led to T-shirts proclaiming, "Don't Whack Our Weiner!"

You know you have a tradition if you can buy a T-shirt of the event. Both "Jump Around" and sausage race T-shirts are available. Both traditions involve crowd participation, albeit one is more aerobic than the other. So which tradition outlasts the other? The sausage race gets the win for this reason: not everyone jumps around during "Jump Around," but everyone gets into the sausage race. In the early years of the 21st century, the sausage race gave Brewers fans something to cheer about. It's unique, and yet a trend-setter. Now, parks in Pittsburgh and Washington—even in Tampa Bay—have their own versions of the sausage race, but there's only one original. It's at Miller Park, and it's the best tradition in Wisconsin sports.

BETTER MASCOT: BERNIE BREWER OR BANGO THE BUCK?

85 This argument is limited to the two professional teams in the state that have mascots. The Bucks have Bango the Buck, and the Brewers have Bernie Brewer. The Packers do not have a mascot.

Bango was born on October 18, 1977, at the season opener against former Buck Kareem Abdul-Jabbar and the Los Angeles Lakers. The name Bango was derived from "the original voice of the Bucks," longtime broadcaster Eddie Doucette, who used to yell, "Bango!" whenever the Bucks hit a big bucket. "Bango" easily won in a fan vote to name the mascot. The modern-day Bango is a lovable deer that appears to hit the gym as often as the players on the court. His athleticism is unparalleled. His acrobatics and thunderous dunks are sometimes more entertaining than the product on the court.

Bernie Brewer originally was human. In the Brewers' first year in Milwaukee, a frustrated 69-year-old Brewer fan named Milt Mason was puzzled that the new baseball team in town did not draw better crowds. In June of 1970, Mason vowed to live on top of the scoreboard until a crowd of 40,000 or better attended a game at County Stadium. Mason did live atop the scoreboard—for a month and a half, until August 16, Bat Day at the ballpark. A crowd of 44,387 watched the Brewers beat the Indians 4–3, and Mason finally came down from his trailer on top of the scoreboard.

The legend of Milt Mason grew until 1973, when the team officially introduced Bernie Brewer inspired by the super fan. There was no trailer for Bernie Brewer—he lived in a chalet on top of a beer barrel in right-center field. When the home team hit a home run, Bernie would slide from his chalet into a beer mug. However, in 1984, the Brewers rebuilt the bleachers and moved Bernie's home into storage for nine years. Bernie did not return regularly until 1993, when he got a major makeover—a new costume and a new look. No longer was Bernie just a guy in lederhosen. When Miller Park was built, the Brewers made sure that Bernie had a new home, as well. He no longer slides into a beer stein—he slides down a bright yellow tornado slide after every Brewers home run.

Bango versus Bernie. No contest—it's Bango all the way. It's tough to vote for Bernie when he did not exist for almost a decade. But even if he did, Bango would still get the vote. Bango is actively involved during in-game promotions—for example, he becomes a pizza delivery guy during the pizza giveaway. The routine in which he dunks off a trampoline is outstanding. During games,

Bango also has a major role in any skit with the Bucks' dance team. It seems like Bango is more spunky and has more personality than Bernie.

You could make the argument that Bernie isn't even the most popular mascot on his own team. He's often overshadowed by the racing sausages. His old chalet doesn't even belong to the Brewers anymore. A local brewery owns it. Bernie does get points for being accused of stealing the opposing team's signals, as he did in 1973. However, Bango the Buck is a better mascot than Bernie Brewer.

WHAT'S THE BEST QUOTE IN WISCONSIN SPORTS (NOT BY VINCE LOMBARDI)?

86 Vince Lombardi is the godfather of Wisconsin sports. His words are legendary, and his quotes are plastered in high school locker rooms all over the state. Lombardi's official website lists dozens of his most famous quotes, and you probably know a few:

"Winning isn't everything, it's the only thing."

"It's not whether you get knocked down, it's whether you get up."

"The harder you work, the harder it is to surrender."

We could go on and on with Lombardi sayings, so let's filter this down to the best quote not uttered by Vince Lombardi. Here are the top five.

5. "WE ARE GOING TO SINK OR SWIM TOGETHER."—LARRY HARRIS

Larry Harris was known as "Likeable" Larry Harris, since he was so accommodating to the local media during his days as the Bucks' general manager. However, some within the Bucks organization had a different view. Desmond Mason was so upset after learning he was traded to the Hornets that he vented on ESPN Radio in Milwaukee and called Larry Harris a "snake in the grass." The same Larry Harris gave his head coach, Terry Porter, a vote of confidence after the 2004–2005 season by putting his arm around Porter and saying, "We are going to sink or swim together." It was one of the more awkward news conferences in Bucks history. Six weeks later, Harris fired Porter, thinking he could replace him with Flip Saunders. That did not happen, and Harris hired Terry Stotts instead. Larry Harris was relieved of his GM duties in March 2008. Both Porter and Harris sank with the Bucks, but not together.

4. "ONLY A DESIGNATED HITTER."—SAL BANDO

Paul Molitor spent his first 15 seasons in Milwaukee playing for the Brewers, and even though he had come off a season where he hit .320, the Brewers were nickel-and-diming him. At one point during negotiations, Brewers general manager Sal Bando referred to Molitor as "only a designated hitter." Frustrated, Molitor accepted a three-year contract with the Toronto Blue Jays worth $13 million. Molitor went on to lead the Blue Jays to the World Series title as the MVP of the Fall Classic. Not bad for just a DH.

253

3. "I LIKE SEASHELLS AND BALLOONS, RIBBONS AND MEDALS, BARE FEET AND WET GRASS."—AL MCGUIRE

Al McGuire, the greatest college basketball coach this state has ever known, often talked about "seashells and balloons." He used the phrase as a coach and then popularized it during his years as a TV analyst. It was one of his favorite sayings that meant joy and satisfaction. McGuire had dozens of pet phrases, but "seashells and balloons" was one of his favorites, and it came to define him. It's a sweet reference to all that is good in life. McGuire was way ahead of his time as a coach and as a basketball analyst. He was always one step ahead of you and yet never forgot about life's simplicities. When McGuire passed away in 2001 from acute leukemia, the lead in his obituary, which appeared in the *Milwaukee Journal-Sentinel*, played off his famous line: "The seashells are broken. The balloons have burst."

2. "THE TRAIN HAS LEFT THE STATION." —MIKE MCCARTHY

Packers head coach Mike McCarthy was at wit's end in August 2008. Football fans, especially those residing in Packer nation, could not understand why the franchise was moving on without Brett Favre. The legendary quarterback had changed his mind, had come out of a short retirement, and now wanted the keys back home. It was a bad breakup that was not easily explained. Like an onion, the Favre story had multiple layers, and the deeper you got, the more it made you want to cry. The best McCarthy could do was use the analogy, "The train has left the station," meaning, "We are moving on without the three-time MVP." As it turned out, the train left the station en route to a 6–10 season for the Packers, with a franchise-record seven losses by four points or less. Favre's Jets finished 9–7 but faded down the stretch, losing four of their final five games as New York missed the playoffs. As for the Aaron Rodgers–Brett Favre comparison, Rodgers threw more touchdowns than Favre in 2008 (28 to 22) and fewer interceptions (13 to 22), yet Favre was voted to the Pro Bowl and Rodgers was not.

1. "WE'RE...JUST A FART IN THE WIND." —RON WOLF

Ron Wolf was livid. The Packers GM had just watched his team lose Super Bowl XXXII, upset by John Elway and the Denver Broncos. It was not supposed to be this way. Football fans were talking about the Packers as the next great NFL dynasty. Instead, Mike Holmgren was outcoached by Mike Shanahan, and the Packers were thoroughly outplayed by the Broncos. Wolf's candid reaction after the game? "We're just a one-year wonder, just a fart in the wind." Wolf was always quotable, but this not only summed up the moment, it also defined a team that could have been so much more.

WHAT'S THE BEST NICKNAME IN WISCONSIN SPORTS?

87 This is purely subjective. Which nickname is your favorite? If you are a Bucks fan, perhaps Bob "the Dobber" Lanier is your guy—or it's "Sir Sid" Moncrief, Glenn "Big Dog" Robinson, Paul "Speed Bump" Mokeskie, or maybe even Brad "the Vanilla Gorilla" Lohaus. Brewers fans have "the Kid," Robin Yount; "the Ignitor," Paul Molitor; and Jim "Gumby" Gantner. Inside the dugout, who knew some veterans called a young Gary Sheffield "Home Plate Face"? Braves fans had Hank Aaron, who had a handful of nicknames to choose from: "Bad Henry," "Hammerin' Hank," or simply "Hammer." Packers fans have "the Golden Boy," Paul Hornung; "the Gravedigger," Gilbert Brown; and—if they dig deep enough—even Donny "Golden Palomino" Anderson. Badgers football fans have Ron "the Great Dayne" and Alan "the Horse" Ameche. One of the best players in Marquette basketball history was George Thompson, aptly dubbed "Brute Force."

For a great nickname to survive the test of time, it has to give you insight about what that player is all about. It also helps if the person is a standout in his or her sport. With that in mind, here are my five favorite Wisconsin sports figure nicknames, in no particular order.

REGGIE WHITE, "THE MINISTER OF DEFENSE"

This is simply one of the most perfect nicknames in sports. The late Reggie White was an ordained minister and was the greatest defensive lineman in NFL history. It's a fantastic nickname for a fantastic player.

JOHNNY "BLOOD" MCNALLY

"Blood" was an alias for Johnny McNally so he could play pro football while still protecting his college eligibility. He was a tough, two-way player who helped the Packers win four NFL championships during the 1920s and 1930s. You would think "Blood" came from one of McNally's vicious tackles or a cut on his face that would not close. Nope. It was a title of a movie, *Blood and Sand,* back in his day. When McNally needed an alias, he told a friend he'd be "Blood" and his friend could take "Sand." The name stuck for 14 NFL seasons that took Johnny "Blood" McNally to the Hall of Fame.

PHIL "SCRAP IRON" GARNER

The former Brewers manager was given this nickname by Hall of Famer Willie Stargell during their playing days in

Pittsburgh. Garner was gritty, intense, and tough and he was a key cog in the "We Are Family" Pirates that won the 1979 World Series. Garner brought those same scrappy characteristics to the Brewers dugout for eight seasons, where he won more games than any manager in team history.

RUFUS "ROADRUNNER" FERGUSON

A shifty running back for the Badgers in the early 1970s, Rufus Ferguson was one of the more talented and colorful players in UW history. He was given the nickname "Roadrunner" by his American Legion baseball coach for his penchant for stealing bases. But it was in Madison where the 5'6", 190-pound Ferguson made his nickname famous. After scoring a key touchdown during a home win against Michigan State in 1972, Ferguson added an end zone dance that instantly became known as "the Roadrunner Shuffle." Ferguson was the first Badger to gain 1,000 yards in a season, and he still ranks in the top 10 on the school's all-time rushing list.

ELROY "CRAZYLEGS" HIRSCH

A Chicago sportswriter gets credit for dubbing Hirsch with this nickname. *Chicago Daily News* writer Francis Powers watched Hirsch scurry 62 yards for a touchdown to help Wisconsin beat the Great Lakes Naval Training Center team in 1942. Hirsch was described as a "demented duck" whose "crazy legs were gyrating in six different directions all at the same time." The name stuck. "Crazylegs" played just one season for the Badgers, leading UW to an 8–1–1 record before being assigned to Michigan while serving in the U.S. Marine Corps. After college and the service, Hirsch played nine years in the NFL with the Los Angeles Rams, and by the time his playing days ended, everyone knew about "Crazylegs." He even enjoyed a short movie career, starring as himself in *Crazylegs, All American* in 1953. Not bad for a kid from Wausau who eventually wound up in both the Pro Football Hall of Fame and the College Football Hall of Fame. Eventually, Hirsch returned to Madison as the school's athletic director and helped start the "Crazylegs Run," which has raised millions of dollars for the UW athletic department since its inception in 1982.

WILL WISCONSIN EVER LAND A NASCAR CUP RACE?

88 The quick and easy answer is no. But it didn't have to be this way. In the mid-1980s, the Milwaukee Mile was on track to host a NASCAR Cup race. A group called GO Racing ran the track at that time and brought a NASCAR Busch Series race to Milwaukee in 1984 and 1985. To compare racing to baseball, the Cup Series (once called the Winston Cup, now the Sprint Cup) is the big leagues, and the Busch Series (now the Nationwide Series) is the triple-A level of the minor leagues. In order to host a Cup race, there were certain improvements that needed to be made to the facility to bring it up to speed. However, GO Racing chose not make those improvements and did not do the minimum required by NASCAR to keep the Busch race. After just two years, NASCAR pulled out of Milwaukee in 1985.

NASCAR returned to Milwaukee in 1993 when the Wisconsin Sports Authority, led by Milwaukee businessman Joe Sweeney, took over the Milwaukee Mile. Since then, the Milwaukee Mile holds a "stand-alone" weekend, meaning it runs a NASCAR Truck Series race on Friday night and a NASCAR Nationwide Series on Saturday, but not a Cup race. Traditionally, the Nationwide race is at the same site as the Cup race on any given weekend, but more and more, there are stand-alone weekends for the minor leagues of NASCAR. No question, it's a big deal to have any level of NASCAR race in your city, but what would have to happen to bring a Cup event to the Milwaukee Mile?

For one, seating capacity at the Mile is too small. The facility holds about 40,000 fans, and NASCAR would want to double that figure. Also, the facility would need major upgrades to meet NASCAR standards. There would need to be construction of a permanent garage area for the race cars, and NASCAR would also need major infrastructure improvements to help run an event at the Cup level. Fan traffic patterns would need to be reconfigured, and officials would have to make the most of the limited space the Mile offers nestled inside the State Fairgrounds. Then there's the facility itself. The Milwaukee Mile is one of the most historic tracks in the world, having been around for more than 100 years. Calling something *historic* is like putting a house up for sale and saying it has character—it's just a nice way of calling it old. Milwaukee Mile officials would have to convince NASCAR officials that the track would be capable of hosting guys like Jimmie Johnson, Jeff Gordon, Dale Earnhardt, Jr., and Matt Kenseth and their huge production staffs. That could possibly mean expansion that would cost millions of dollars and require space now occupied by homes and businesses. Finally, there is the parking issue. The Milwaukee Mile is not set up to host a Cup race, since it doesn't have built-in parking for spectators. The Mile would have to work out a deal with Miller Park and shuttle fans back and forth.

The Milwaukee Mile had its chance in the mid-1980s. NASCAR was expanding, searching for untapped markets to showcase its stars. Milwaukee would have been a perfect stop for the Cup Series. Now, that time has passed. NASCAR's Cup Series has stops in Chicago, Kansas City, and Indianapolis, as well as its regular stop in the Detroit area. Adding Milwaukee, with its historic facility, would not make sense when there are other options so close by, especially the newer facilities in Chicago and Kansas City, plus the historic Brickyard in Indianapolis. It would take millions and millions of dollars just to get back on the NASCAR Cup radar, and the investment would be a very risky one.

Wisconsin has one of the most underrated and passionate racing fan bases in the country. The Milwaukee Mile attracts thousands of race fans every summer for its NASCAR weekend and its IndyCar race. The short tracks in smaller communities throughout the state are staples of Wisconsin recreation. Enjoy what we have here—many states can't even come close to what Wisconsin has on the track. Don't take it for granted, either, since you never know how long the big boys will continue racing in the state, even if it's only at the Nationwide and Truck Series levels.

HITS AND MISSES

WHO'S THE BEST DRIVER IN WISCONSIN SPORTS HISTORY?

89 America's Dairyland has produced some of the best drivers in the NASCAR Cup Series. Alan Kulwicki blazed the NASCAR trail for Cup regulars like Matt Kenseth, Johnny Sauter, Scott Wimmer, and Travis Kvapil. And let's not forget about Dick Trickle, owner of 1,200 reported short-track wins. Trickle won the 1989 NASCAR Rookie of the Year at age 48. Wausau's Dave Marcis still holds the record for most starts at the Daytona 500—he won five Cup races, and in 1975 he finished second in the points standings to Richard Petty.

Then there's Ted Musgrave, who was born in Waukegan, Illinois, but moved across the border so he could race more. Musgrave planted roots in Franklin while he worked his way up the ladder en route to becoming the 2005 NASCAR Truck Series champion.

Wisconsin is also the home of Richie Bickle, veteran of both the Nationwide and Truck Series. Short-track legends like Tom Reffner of Rudolph built the state's reputation for hard-nosed, hard-working drivers who'd race six nights a week and sometimes twice on Sundays. Steve Carlson of West Salem, who won nine national late-model touring championships, still battles the young bucks around short tracks, even though he's in his 50s. The short-track battles between Miles "the Mouse" Melius of Slinger and Billy "the Cat" Johnson are legendary. Joe Shear, Al Schill, Conrad Morgan, Terry Baldry, and Lowell Bennett are just a handful of standouts who make up the backbone of Wisconsin's racing past. But the best of the best boils down to two drivers—Matt Kenseth and Alan Kulwicki.

Matt Kenseth will be forever compared with the late Alan Kulwicki, as both drivers are the only two from Wisconsin to win NASCAR's biggest prize, the Cup championship. Even though the two share the title of former champions, they could not be more different.

Kulwicki grew up in West Allis, minutes from the Milwaukee Mile, and attended a private Catholic high school, Milwaukee Pius. He got his college degree at UWM and then worked as an engineer in order to fund his racing dream. His education helped him master the physics of the sport, and he was known as a quick thinker on the track. Legend has it that Kulwicki could calculate gas mileage as he was weaving in and out of traffic as he raced. He could also foreshadow shortcomings among his competitors. For example, if he saw low tire pressure on another car, he would radio to his guys to hustle over to that car's pit so when the tire did blow, leading to a race-ending wreck, his crew could buy the remaining tires from them at a discounted price. He was focused, intense, and relentless in his pursuit of racing at the highest level—so much so that Kulwicki surprised many when he moved his operations from Wisconsin to North Carolina in the 1980s to take on the boys from Tobacco Road head on.

Kulwicki won the Cup title in 1992, in the final race, because he knew exactly how many laps he needed to lead the race to earn crucial bonus points that gave him the title. He won the season championship by just 10 points—at the time, the slimmest margin in NASCAR history. Kulwicki thrilled fans after winning races by performing his "Polish victory lap." Instead of going counterclockwise, as drivers do when they race, Kulwicki went against the grain, going clockwise around the track so his fans could see him on the driver's side as he celebrated. It was classic Kulwicki to do things his way, and many saw this celebration as the precursor to the modern-day doughnuts, spinouts, and backflips seen weekly at NASCAR's highest level. Tragically, Kulwicki's life was cut short when his small plane crashed in April 1993.

Eleven years after Kulwicki won his title, another Wisconsin-bred driver rode down Victory Lane. Matt Kenseth was born in Cambridge and cut his teeth in his father's garage. He convinced his dad, Roy, to buy him a race car when he was 13, but part of the deal was that Matt would work on his dad's race car until Matt was old enough to race himself. Matt grew up on the short tracks of Wisconsin, taking on guys like Bickle, Trickle, and Shear. Money was constantly an issue. Kenseth didn't have much, but he kept grinding away until he caught his big break—his old nemesis on the track, Robbie Reiser, called him in 1997 to drive for Reiser's then–Bush Series ride. From there, NASCAR veteran Mark Martin befriended Kenseth, and the young driver quickly became a sponge, soaking up anything and everything he could to become a better driver. Martin convinced team owner Jack Rousch that Kenseth had what it took to become a great NASCAR driver. Martin was instrumental in Rousch keeping the Reiser-Kenseth team intact when the two moved into Rousch Racing's Cup stable full time in 2000. Kenseth won his Winston Cup title in 2003, despite winning just one race. His consistency built up a points lead that led to a ho-hum finish to the racing season. It was so anticlimactic, NASCAR then made what many consider to be the "Kenseth Rule" and changed the format of how the championship is decided. The following year, NASCAR created its own playoff system, the "Chase for the Championship," which reset the points standings for the final 10 races of the season. In February 2009, Kenseth added to his legacy, becoming the first Wisconsin driver to win the "Super Bowl of stock-car racing," the Daytona 500. The following week, Kenseth became the first driver in 12 years to win the first two races of the Cup season, taking the checkered flag at the Auto Club 500 in Fontana, California.

Kulwicki and Kenseth are similar in they are both from Wisconsin and have both won championships, but that's about it. Kulwicki was his own boss in a simpler time in NASCAR, while Kenseth is part of corporate NASCAR, a piece of the puzzle that drives hard and fair but rarely ruffles any feathers. If you are comparing the two strictly on the numbers, here's food for thought. Kulwicki started a total of 207 races on NASCAR's Cup circuit, so in comparing Kenseth's first 207 races to Kulwicki's career, Kenseth dominates almost every category. Kenseth has the edge in victories (nine to five), top-five finishes (Kenseth 43, Kulwicki 38), and top-10 finishes (Kenseth 90, Kulwicki 75).

But Kulwicki was a master at qualifying. In fact, Dale Earnhardt, Sr., used the nickname "Quickie" for Kulwicki, since the owner-driver ran so fast during qualifying. Kulwicki won 24 career pole positions to just one for Kenseth in his first 207 starts. (Kenseth would win his second pole and his 10th race in his 208th start at Michigan in 2005.) Through his first 207 races, Kenseth led 5,667 of the 58,340 laps he completed, meaning he led 9.7 percent of the time he was on the track. Kulwicki, meanwhile, led just 4.4 percent of the time (2,686 of the 61,693 laps he completed on the track).

"Kulwicki was a local hero in every way," says Jim Tretow, vice president of media and communications for the Milwaukee Mile, who watched both Kulwicki and Kenseth work through the ranks. Kulwicki's death in 1993 came as a shock to race fans everywhere—the sitting NASCAR points champion was tragically killed in a plane crash. In fact, later in 1993, Kenseth won the Alan Kulwicki Memorial Race in a super-late model at Slinger Speedway shortly after Kulwicki's death.

As good a driver as Kenseth is, he's not going to stir the pot. He's not one to seek out attention—and that's not a knock, by any means. That's who he is. Kenseth is a racing lifer who is polite with the media and connects with his fans but isn't one to go to for a controversial sound bite. "Matt's a clean, hard-nosed race car driver," says Tretow. "He's not going to spin you out on purpose. He's consistent and that consistency won him a championship in 2003." Kenseth finished in the top ten 25 times during his championship season.

Kulwicki may be more revered by Wisconsin race fans, but Kenseth is the better driver. Tretow is convinced that if Kulwicki were still alive, he would be a car owner but no longer would be a driver. Kenseth will drive a race car as long as he has a ride. It's a title that's underrated and overlooked, but Matt Kenseth is the best driver to come out of the great racing state of Wisconsin.

WHO'S THE BEST GOLFER IN WISCONSIN HISTORY?

90 Summers in Wisconsin are many things, but long is not one of them. It's remarkable, then, to consider all of the outstanding golfers to come out of the state. Wisconsin has a rich tradition of excellence on the links. Skip Kendall, J. P. Hayes, Bob Brue, and Mark Wilson all found success at one time or another on the PGA Tour. When talking about the best golfer in state history, it's a three-man debate between Steve Stricker, Jerry Kelly, and Andy North.

Stricker grew up in Edgerton and Kelly in Madison. The two golfers have combined for more than $40 million and counting in career earnings. They've each won big tournaments—Stricker won the Barclays, Kelly won the Sony Open. Both men have won the Western Open. Stricker finished second to Tiger Woods at the inaugural FedEx Cup in 2007. He also has the unique honor of winning the PGA's Comeback Player of the Year Award twice. Both men have represented the United States in international competition. But neither have what Andy North has—a major championship—and North has two of them.

North was born in Thorpe and grew up in the Madison area. He is one of 16 men to win multiple U.S. Opens. He won his first at Cherry Hills, Colorado, in 1978, and his second at Oakland Hills, Michigan, in 1985. Like Stricker and Kelly, as a player North has flown under the radar, for the most part. Many golf fans remember T. C. "Two-Chip" Chen losing the 1985 U.S. Open as much as they recall North winning it. Chen had the misfortune of striking the ball twice out of the rough on the fifth hole of the final round with a four-stroke lead. Chen wound up taking a quadruple-bogey eight and allowed the field back into the tournament. North took full advantage of the opportunity and beat Chen and two others by a stroke.

North won three PGA tournaments during his career—two of them U.S. Opens. However, if not for physical limitations, North may have won more. Golf fans might wonder how many tournaments North would have won had it not been for his bad knees, elbow, and neck. He's endured more than a dozen surgeries, including a handful to beat skin cancer. Most golf fans recognize North as much, if not more, for his TV work over the years on ABC and ESPN as for his playing career.

North has won more money on the Champions (Seniors) Tour than he did on the PGA Tour. However, success in golf isn't all about money. Tiger Woods will be the first to tell you that it's about the majors. North owns two—that's two more than any other Wisconsin golfer, and that is why Andy North is the greatest golfer in state history.

WHAT WAS WISCONSIN'S MOST EMBARRASSING SPORTS MOMENT?

91 America's Dairyland has seen its share of lowlights over the years: the Brewers' 14 years without a winning season; the Badgers' 23-game winless streak in football in the late 1960s; the Packers under Forrest Gregg; Bob Dukiet's Marquette basketball teams; Steve Yoder's basketball teams at UW; the Don Morton era, also at UW. Take your pick—there are plenty of options to choose from. But if you had to choose just one event, one embarrassing moment in the state's sports history, there's one that stands above—or below—all others.

The 2002 Major League Baseball All-Star Game was supposed to be puffed-chest time for Commissioner Bud Selig. It should have been a signature moment in his tenure. After all, he brought baseball back to Milwaukee in the early 1970s. He owned the Brewers until becoming baseball's leader, but as commissioner he still made sure that Miller Park was built, and this was the evening to showcase his gem. This was his night. But on this steamy July evening in 2002 in Milwaukee, Selig realized his worst fears.

First of all, the 2002 All-Star Game will be forever known as the pinnacle of the steroid era. Anyone who was in attendance for the Home Run Derby the night before the Midsummer Classic could tell that these men weren't men. They were superhuman, energized by science. Jason Giambi won the Home Run Derby, but most fans remember Sammy Sosa knocking a ball out of Miller Park, as well as hitting the .300 Club in the upper deck of left field. The derby was a living cartoon, a live video game.

In the game itself, the San Francisco Giants' Barry Bonds hit a home run and was in position to win the game's Most Valuable Player Award if the National League could hold on to win the game. Bonds watched the later innings in street clothes outside the NL's locker room with his family in tow, waiting for the game to end so he could pick up his award. But there was one big problem—the game didn't end. In fact, it still hasn't. The American League took the lead in the seventh, and Bonds left the park in disgust shortly thereafter. The fact that Bonds didn't even stay until the conclusion of the game signified what the result of the All-Star Game meant to players then: very little.

The game went back and forth before the AL tied it for good in the eighth. The score remained tied into the 11th inning, when both teams ran out of players. Both managers, Bob Brenly and Joe Torre, met with Commissioner Selig to discuss what to do next. There was only one option—to end the game. So the 73rd All-Star Game ended after 11 innings in a 7–7 tie.

The sellout crowd of 41,871 was beyond angry. Those in the stands screamed, "Let them play! Let them play!" Selig was stuck—his All-Star teams were both out of players, and he knew it. The lasting image of that night is Selig lifting his hands heavenward as if to say, "What can I do?"

If there's a silver lining to the story, it's this: Shortly after the tie, Major League Baseball announced that the All-Star Game would no longer be treated as an exhibition, and the game's winner would secure home-field advantage for its representative team in the World Series. The thought was that if there was truly something to play for other than just pride, everyone—fans, players, and coaches—would treat the game more seriously. Selig also expanded the rosters for the All-Star Game, hoping what happened in his hometown back in 2002 would never happen again.

WHICH WAS THE BETTER SEASON FINALE, PACKERS 2003 OR BREWERS 2008?

92 "Let's go Cardinals! Let's go Cardinals!"—Packers fans at Lambeau Field, December 28, 2003.

"Let's go Marlins! Let's go Marlins!"—Brewers fans at Miller Park, September 28, 2008.

Does the name Nathan Poole ring a bell? His career numbers won't wow you—34 catches, 418 yards, and two touchdowns in his four-year NFL career. But for Packers fans, Poole ranks right up there with the Steelers' Yancey Thigpen as their favorite wide receiver who did not wear green and gold. Thigpen dropped a sure touchdown on Christmas Eve in 1995 that gave the Packers a division title. Poole caught a pass in 2003 to not only give the Packers a division title, but also to knock the Vikings out of a playoff spot.

Green Bay was in the process of drilling the Denver Broncos 31–3 on the final afternoon of the 2003 regular season. However, in a twist of fate, the Packers would be left out of the NFL postseason party if the Vikings held on to beat the Cardinals in Arizona. The Vikings blew a 12-point lead in the final two minutes. Poole's catch in the end zone for the Cardinals finished off the comeback and ended Minnesota's playoff hopes. At Lambeau Field, the news of Poole's heroics spread like wildfire at the two-minute warning. When word filtered down to the sidelines, Packers players were hugging and waving towels, and a few even went to the first row to exchange high fives with fans. It was a surreal moment.

Poole received a hero's welcome a week later. He and his wife, Neville, were the guests of Green Bay mayor Jim Schmitt for the Packers' Wild Card game against the Seahawks at Lambeau Field. Poole was mobbed at the airport in Green Bay, and he received a key to the city for the biggest catch of his career.

In 2008, the Brewers needed final-day heroics, as well. Milwaukee was tied with the New York Mets for the National League wild card with one game to play. At Miller Park, C. C. Sabathia pitched another brilliant game against the Cubs, while Ryan Braun provided the offense in the eighth inning with a two-run, tie-breaking home run that electrified the sellout crowd. The Brewers beat the Cubs 3–1 but had to sit and wait on the outcome of the Mets–Marlins game in New York. Miller Park then turned into the world's largest sports bar, with 44,000 watching the Mets–Marlins game on the Jumbotron in center field.

Florida held on to knock out the Mets, ending the Brewers 26-year playoff drought.

The scene at Miller Park was amazing. Brewers owner Mark Attanasio, like many of the Brewers players, decided to grow a lucky beard and avoided shaving during the final week of the season. There he was with his playoff beard and goggles to protect his eyes from champagne—it was a sight to be seen. Brewers players poured back onto the field after the Mets' loss to celebrate with the fans. Some sprayed champagne into the crowd, and the fans loved every minute of it. There wasn't a dry eye in the house, whether from the bubbly or from fans bubbling over in disbelief. The Milwaukee Brewers would play baseball in October. It was an incredible scene.

Both afternoons were truly special. Both the Packers and the Brewers needed help on the final day of the regular season to make the playoffs. However, the Brewers' celebration was a little different. The Packers were used to going to the playoffs. The Brewers were used to watching the playoffs on TV. The fact that the Packers had sneaked their way into the postseason was exciting but not a moment for the ages. The Brewers winning their way in after their roller-coaster regular season was one of those "You had to be there" sports moments that Brewers fans will be retelling to generations to come.

WHO'S THE BEST WISCONSIN HIGH SCHOOL FOOTBALL PLAYER IN HISTORY?

93

The beauty of this argument is that you could get more than a dozen answers, depending on which part of the state you are standing in when you ask the question. More than a handful of players merit consideration, and depending on how old you are and where you grew up watching prep football, your answer could be completely different than the next person's answer. So, let's break up the debate into two categories: the best player in the last 20 years, and the best player, period.

John Clay of Racine Park High School is the best football player in the last 20 years. At 6'2" and 220 pounds, Clay was bigger than most of the defensive linemen trying to tackle him in high school, and yet he could outrun defensive backs. In the fall of 2005, Clay's junior year at Park was one for the ages. Even though he missed two games and part of a third with an ankle injury, he still rushed for 2,032 yards and an average of 12.2 yards per carry.

He scored 30 touchdowns, which included eight scores on runs of 65 yards or more. Clay rushed for a Division 1 record 259 yards in the state championship game, as Park beat Wisconsin Rapids. He was so impressive that former Badgers lineman Jamie Vanderveldt simply wrote, "He's Good" on the telestrator during a commercial break after a Clay touchdown. Enough said. The only thing holding Clay back from taking the title as the greatest prep player in state history was a somewhat disappointing senior season in the fall of 2006 in which Park failed to make the playoffs. Clay was still named an All-American and went on to play college ball at the University of Wisconsin.

There are possible arguments for a number of great high school football players in the state. Future Hall of Famer Dave Casper, who played on an undefeated Chilton team that did not give up a single point in 1969 is one. Running back Rocky Bleier was the State Player of the Year twice in the early 1960s in his days at Appleton Xavier. There's also Jim Bertelsen of Hudson, who went on to lead Texas to a collegiate national championship in 1969; Wausau's Elroy Hirsch, before he became "Crazylegs"; Jim Melka of West Allis Central; and David Greenwood of Park Falls, who could be the greatest all-around high school athlete in state history. Tom Oates, a longtime columnist for the *Wisconsin State Journal*, says that in 1989, in the Division 4 State Championship Game, Southern Door's Jim Flanigan "dominated the game both offensively and defensively like no player I've ever seen."

Let's also not forget standouts like John Anderson of Waukesha South; Brian Calhoun of Oak Creek; Brent Moss of Racine Park; and Joe Thomas of Brookfield Central. But when all is said and done, most football historians in the state will vote for Alan "the Horse" Ameche of Kenosha as the best football player in state history. Ameche was 5'11" and 215, and in his day, like Clay, he was bigger than most linemen he played against. He helped Kenosha (now Bradford) High School to an undefeated season in 1950 as his team scored more touchdowns than the opposition scored points. Interestingly, Ameche's teammate at Kenosha was Tom Braatz, who would go on to become the vice president of player personnel for the Packers in the 1980s. The 1950 team could give Casper's 1969 Chilton team a run for its money as the greatest team in state history. Ameche's toughness was the thing that stood out. He was a bruiser, which carried over to his Heisman-winning career at Wisconsin and then on to the NFL. There, he helped win the NFL championship for the Colts, scoring the winning touchdown in overtime to beat the New York Giants in what's now known as "the Greatest Game Ever Played." Ameche was one of a kind and is the best high school football player the state has ever seen.

WHO'S THE BEST WISCONSIN HIGH SCHOOL BASKETBALL PLAYER IN HISTORY?

94

BOYS

Just like the best prep football player debate, this question can be asked in two parts. One, who was the greatest player the state's ever seen? Two, who was the greatest player in the last 20 years? The answer to the latter is Cassville's Sam Okey. The versatile swingman dominated prep basketball like no other player since 1990. He helped little Cassville High School to back-to-back state titles in his junior and senior seasons.

Okey stood 6'7" and would toy with opponents, especially since Cassville played in the small-school division in Wisconsin. He had moxie, too. As a senior at the state tournament in Madison, Okey blocked a shot and then got the ball back for one of his patented, left-handed dunks. At the next whistle, Okey glanced over to the TV table where the announcers were calling the game to a statewide audience, smiled, and winked as if to say, "This is too easy"—which it was for Sam Okey in high school. He was a man among boys. Okey graduated from Cassville in 1995 ranked fourth on the state's all-time scoring list with 2,539 points. After making a splash as the Big Ten's freshman of the year in 1996, Okey never realized his potential at UW. He did not see eye to eye with UW head coach Dick Bennett, and he wound up transferring to Iowa in January 1998. Okey's collegiate career may have been a disappointment, but as a prep player he was the best one after 1990.

The answer to the question of who is the state's best high school player ever is almost unanimous—Joe Wolf of Kohler, from 1979 to 1983. Wolf was a 6'10" center but wasn't limited to banging inside—he could also step out and hit the midrange jumper. He could do it all. In his career, Wolf averaged 22 points a game. In his junior and senior seasons, he averaged more than 30 points a game. He led tiny Kohler High to three Class "C" championships in his four seasons. In his prep career, Wolf led Kohler to an 88–11 record. In 2005, Cliff Christl of the *Milwaukee Journal-Sentinel* put together a list of the greatest prep basketball players in state history, and Joe Wolf was at the top of the list. The names that Wolf beat out are impressive: Tony Bennett of Green Bay Preble; John Johnson of Milwaukee Messmer; Jim Chones of Racine Park and Racine St. Catherine's; Fred Brown and Clarence Sherrod of Milwaukee Lincoln; Wayne Kreklow of Neenah; Rick Olson of Madison LaFollette; Rhinelander's John Kotz; Wausaukee's Anthony Pieper; Kenosha St. Joe's Nick Van

283

Exel; Wauwatosa East's Devin Harris; and Cassville's Sam Okey to name a few. Wolf could go to college anywhere in the country and eventually chose North Carolina, where he had a standout collegiate career before a solid career in the NBA.

GIRLS

When looking at the list of great female basketball players in Wisconsin prep history, one name jumps out—Janesville Parker's Mistie Bass. She's the only girls' basketball player in state history to win the Miss Basketball Award more than once, and she won it three times in her career. She was as dominant a player during her time at Janesville Parker as any in state history—boys or girls. Bass, a center, helped Janesville Parker reach the state tournament all four years she was in school, and she helped the Vikings win back-to-back Division 1 state titles her sophomore and junior seasons. In her career, Bass averaged 19.1 points, 11.7 rebounds, and 3.8 blocks per game. She was a *USA Today* first team All-American her senior season and played in the inaugural McDonald's Girls All-American Game. Bass went on to an outstanding collegiate career at Duke, during which time she got married and was known as Mistie Williams.

There have been some other incredible girls' high school basketball players in Wisconsin: names like Heidi Bunek at Milwaukee Pius; Niagara's Anna DeForge; Middleton's

Angie Halbleib; South Shore's Jolene Anderson; Stevens Point's Janel McCarville; and Sonja Henning, Keisha Anderson, and LaTonya Sims of Racine Park. But the best of the bunch was Mistie Bass of Janesville Parker.

WHAT'S THE BEST HIGH SCHOOL BASKETBALL GAME IN STATE HISTORY?

95

It's one of the top moments in state history, and it's been called "the shot heard 'round Wisconsin." It was the 1969 WIAA Boys' Basketball Championship Game, and it was before divisional play gave Wisconsin multiple state champions. Beloit played Neenah in a classic. Beloit was down two with the ball and had to go the length of the UW Field House floor to tie the game. Junior LaMont Weaver had enough to time to heave up a desperation 55-footer that banked in to send the game to overtime. (This was before the three-point line was invented.) Then Weaver hit a couple of clutch free throws late in double-overtime to help Beloit beat Neenah 80–79 for the state championship. A little-known tidbit about that game—one of Neenah's reserves that day was Craig Leipold, who later would go on to own the Nashville Predators and then the Minnesota Wild of the NHL.

How big was the Weaver shot? In 1999, the *Milwaukee Journal-Sentinel* ranked it 19th on the list of greatest Wisconsin sports moments of the 20th century, ahead of the Brewers' 1982 World Series appearance and UW's Alan Ameche winning the Heisman Trophy. It was the most famous shot in Wisconsin history in the greatest prep basketball game this state has ever seen.

WHO'S THE GREATEST WISCONSIN OLYMPIAN IN HISTORY?

96 Wisconsin has an underrated group of Olympic champions. Madison's Mark Johnson and Bob Suter led the 1980 U.S. Olympic hockey team to its "Miracle on Ice." Waukesha gymnast Paul Hamm and West Allis speedskater Dan Jansen both won emotional gold medals.

One of the earliest Olympic groundbreakers was track star Ralph Metcalfe, who grew up in Chicago but went to Marquette. Metcalfe won a gold medal with Jesse Owens in the 4 x 100-meter relay in the 1936 Olympics, with the shadow of Adolf Hitler looming in Berlin. In all, Metcalfe won one gold, two silvers, and a bronze medal in two trips to the Olympics. Speedskater Bonnie Blair was born in Champaign, Illinois, but Wisconsin adopted her after she moved to the Milwaukee area to be closer to her training facility. Blair finished her skating career as the most decorated American female winter Olympian of all time, winning five gold medals and one bronze in three trips to the Winter Games. Swimmer Jim Montgomery brought three golds and one bronze back home to Madison after the 1976 Summer Games in Montreal. Montgomery was the first man to break the 50-second barrier in the 100-meter freestyle. However, the greatest Olympian from Wisconsin is speedskater Eric Heiden.

Heiden turned in one of the greatest individual Olympic performances this side of Michael Phelps and Mark Spitz. At the 1980 Winter Games, Heiden accomplished something no man had done before him—he won every men's event in speedskating. He won five gold medals in nine days—in the 500-meter, the 1,000-meter, the 1,500-meter, the 5,000-meter, and the 10,000-meter races. This incredible feat was overshadowed a bit, thanks to the U.S. hockey team and its remarkable upset of the Russians. What should not be forgotten is that Heiden set four Olympic records in Lake Placid, New York, in 1980, and set one new world record.

Remarkably, Heiden never reached superstar status in the United States, even though he was an icon all over Europe. But Heiden has said many times that he never got into skating for the fame. He once said that if he wanted to be famous, he would have kept playing hockey. Heiden was not one for the spotlight and decided to retire from speedskating after his magical run in 1980. ESPN recognized Heiden in 1999, ranking him No. 46 in *ESPN's SportsCentury 50 Greatest Athletes of the 20th Century*. He was the lone speedskater on the list. In the 56 years that the United States competed in Olympic speedskating prior to 1980, Americans won nine gold medals. Eric Heiden won five in a week and a half.

97 Even though Mark Johnson was arguably the best player in college hockey, he did not know if he'd make the 1980 Olympic team, since his dad, Bob, was the head coach at Wisconsin, and the Olympic coach, Herb Brooks, who was the head coach at Minnesota, were bitter rivals. Johnson did make the team and made the difference in the greatest upset in Olympic history when the USA beat the Soviet Union 4–3 in the medal round in what's now known as the "Miracle on Ice." Johnson scored two of the four goals by the United States, including one to tie the game as the horn sounded to end the first period. His second goal tied the game 3–3 in the third period, which eventually set up Mike Eruzione's historic game-winner.

The mighty Soviets had won eight of the previous nine Olympic hockey gold medals, including the last four, and they took a 21-game Olympic winning streak into the game against the United States Yet a team of upstart college kids, which included Johnson's UW teammate Bob Suter, was able to pull off arguably the greatest upset in sports history. It wasn't just a hockey win; it was a victory against a world superpower in the middle of the Cold War. It was a shot in the arm that gave the American psyche a boost it desperately needed in the wake of Vietnam and Watergate. The spunky Americans beat the powerful USSR, and Madison native Mark Johnson was a huge reason why.

Speedskater Dan Jansen's emotional gold-medal win in his final race at the Winter Games in 1994 was a memory for the ages. Paul Hamm's individual gold medal in the men's all-around gymnastics in 2004 was terrific, even with the scoring controversy that surrounded the victory. However, the best Olympic moment belongs to one of the greatest sports moments in American history—the one that made us believe in miracles.

WHO HAD THE BEST EXIT IN WISCONSIN SPORTS HISTORY?

98 There's a reason why people hate to say good-bye. It's never easy, especially in sports. It's tough to walk away. Rarely is there a clean, classy good-bye but there are exceptions.

Brett Favre made the original list—however, he could be the first athlete to go from best exit to worst exit after his return to football following a four-month retirement. Favre left the NFL the first time on such a high note, helping the Packers to within one play of a return trip to the Super Bowl. But the competitive fire still burned in Favre, which set the wheels in motion for one of the strangest sequences of events in NFL history. So Favre gets "traded" from the best-exit list to the worst.

Speaking of Favre, one of the stadiums where he built his legacy begins the best good-bye list. From the Braves to the Brewers, County Stadium was the home to professional baseball in Milwaukee from 1953 to 2000. It wasn't Wrigley Field or Yankee Stadium, but for generations of baseball fans in Wisconsin, County Stadium was home. Almost 65 million fans walked through the turnstiles at the old ballpark.

County Stadium dropped its curtain after its final show on September 28, 2000. The Brewers lost to the Cincinnati Reds 8–1 as the final score to the final game at the old ballpark. However, aside from back-to-back trips to the World Series in the late 1950s, the final game was County Stadium's finest moment. Baseball legends like Hank Aaron, Warren Spahn, Robin Yount, Paul Molitor, and Rollie Fingers were there. The Packers called County Stadium their part-time home until 1994, and the Green and Gold were represented by Willie Davis, Fuzzy Thurston, and Jim Taylor.

Yount roared into the ceremony on his Harley, much like he did 28 years prior, during the Brewers' glory days. Former and current players lined the field from home plate to the center field wall. Bernie Brewer lowered County Stadium's American flag one final time before handing the wrapped flag from one player to the next—at last, Yount passed the flag to Mark Loretta, the Brewers' senior active player.

The capper was Bob Uecker, the Brewers' legendary broadcaster. His farewell speech to the old stadium is one that lives on long after the wrecking ball hit. Uecker said, "It was here that boys became men and men became champions and champions became legends...We will never forget you. For what was, will always be. So long, old friend." And with that, the lights went out forever at County Stadium.

The best individual exit has to be one in which the subject leaves on top. Favre lost his final game with the

Packers, and Yount lost his with the Brewers. The two who went out on top were speedskater Dan Jansen and Marquette basketball coach Al McGuire.

Just four games into the 1976–1977 season, McGuire knew it was time. So on December 17, 1976, McGuire let his intentions be known—his 13th season coaching the Warriors would be his last. Marquette entered the 1977 NCAA Tournament with a 20–7 record, far from being the favorite. However, McGuire inspired his team to rip off five straight victories to win it all. The image of the head coach weeping in the closing moments of Marquette's win in the title game against North Carolina says it all: McGuire, head in hands, wearing his emotions literally on his sleeves. In classic "Al" form, his famous quote after winning it all was, "It's not often a kid from the street gets to touch the silk lace." McGuire went out on top.

Never has one man gotten more out of one gold medal than Dan Jansen. His Olympic performance in 1994 was one for the storybooks. It was a script perfect for Hollywood featuring a leading man from West Allis.

Jansen set eight world records in speedskating, but the one goal that was most elusive to him was an Olympic gold medal. He finished fourth in 1984, missing out on a medal by 0.16 seconds. In 1988, on the morning of his first race, Jansen learned that his sister Jane had lost her battle with leukemia. Then Jansen fell during his race later that day. Four days later, while skating at a world-record pace,

Jansen fell again. Four years later, in 1992, Jansen was again disappointed, staying on his feet but coming up short.

Lillehammer, Norway, in 1994, was Jansen's final chance at an Olympic medal. In his first race, disaster struck again, as Jansen fell during the finals of the 500 meters. Four days later, in his ultimate opportunity for Olympic glory, Jansen saved his best for last, winning the 1,000 meters. On the medal stand, tears in his eyes, Jansen looked heavenward and had this message for his sister: "This is for you, Jane. I love you."

Both exits by McGuire and Jansen were emotional, but which was better? McGuire's exit was better for the reason that it was unexpected. Not many predicted that Marquette would make the run they did in the NCAA Tournament. Jansen, meanwhile, was expected to contend for medals in four separate Olympics. This is not to take away from anything Jansen accomplished—his exit was one of the great moments of the 1994 Olympic Games. But you can still see McGuire's head in his hands as he sobbed tears of joy. It was a terrific moment and the best individual exit in Wisconsin sports history.

WHO HAD THE WORST EXIT IN WISCONSIN SPORTS HISTORY?

99 All sports figures want to go out on top, to leave their sports at the top of their game. Packers fans know all too well that the best example of leaving on top was Broncos quarterback John Elway. The legendary quarterback is one of the rare few to retire not only a winner, but after back-to-back seasons winning two Super Bowl rings—the first at the expense of the Green Bay Packers in Super Bowl XXXII. Unfortunately, Brett Favre's exit from Green Bay was nothing like Elway's good-bye. Favre's farewell was surrounded with disappointment first on the "frozen tundra" then from the cold chill from the Packers front office as he was sent packing to New York.

Brett Favre lost his final game as a Packer, one step away from the Super Bowl, in the NFC Championship Game. What's worse is that Favre was a big reason why Green Bay lost on that frigid Sunday night in late January 2008. Two months later, Favre shocked many in football by deciding to retire after 17 NFL seasons.

March 6, 2008. Lambeau Field. Favre's announcement and follow-up news conference lasted more than an hour. It was just Brett at a table in front of a plain black backdrop with simple Packers logos—no advertisements—and a throwback microphone to speak into: an old-school microphone for an old-school legend. It was a classic setting. Much like his playing career, the announcement was unrehearsed and from the heart. Much like his playing career, parts made you laugh and parts made you cry. Favre said, while choking back tears, "I hope that every penny that they've spent on me they know was money well spent." It was fascinating theater. If this was it for Favre, it would go down as one of the best exits in Wisconsin sports history. Unfortunately, this wasn't good-bye; it was good-bye for four months.

Sports fans had gotten used to the "Will he or won't he?" debate surrounding Favre over the years, but since he was such an incredible talent and a galvanizing force for the Packers, fans tolerated his waffling. However, his return in the summer of 2008 split Packers fans in half. Some say he should have just kept his word and stayed retired. Others say Favre had every right to change his mind, and such a talent should be appreciated. In the end, Favre was traded to the Jets in one of the most awkward weeks in NFL history. Favre's good-bye to Packers fans was a quick wave as he got onto his private plane with his wife, Deanna, ready to fly off and become a Jet. But Favre definitely has company in the awkward-exit department.

Bobby Knight made an awkward exit in Madison in April of 1968 before he ever officially took over as head coach at Wisconsin. Upset that word of his hiring had leaked out before details were finalized, Knight nixed the whole deal, returned to Army, and later haunted the Badgers for decades as head coach at Indiana.

Speaking of college basketball and Indiana, Tom Crean spent nine seasons at Marquette, restoring basketball there to the highest level and guiding MU into a new era as a member in the Big East Conference. However, year in and year out, Crean's name was linked to high-profile vacancies in college basketball. Kentucky, Illinois, West Virginia, Ohio State—even Indiana, after Mike Davis was let go—had openings during Crean's tenure at Marquette. Every rumor was just that—a rumor. When Indiana sent Kelvin Sampson packing, for once Crean's name wasn't prominently mentioned on websites and message boards as a candidate. That's when he left. There was an emotional team meeting at Crean's Mequon home the night he accepted the job. "It's Indiana," the Crean camp would say. Marquette players were confused and crushed. Some would not or could not talk to the media gathered outside the basketball offices on campus. There was no warning—just an opening at one of the most prestigious college basketball programs in the country. "It's Indiana." It was one of those once-in-a-lifetime chances.

Crean took it, but unfortunately, his players and Marquette fans were blindsided.

Badgers fans knew Barry Alvarez would step down after the 2005 football season. The school planned a ceremony to honor their most successful head coach in program history after its final home game of the season. Unfortunately, UW forgot to tell Iowa that they were supposed to roll over. On November 12, 2005, the Badgers were beaten by the Hawkeyes 20–10 in a driving rainstorm at Camp Randall. After the loss, Alvarez reluctantly played along with the pomp and circumstance, complete with speeches from dignitaries and a farewell video, with his family surrounding him on stage. All the while, the residue of a loss to the team he loved beating decorated his face. It was an awkward evening that celebrated the coaching career of a man who was too ticked off to enjoy it. But this was an exit for the home fans at Camp Randall; in the end, Alvarez got the last laugh, winning his final game as his Badgers pulled off a major upset, knocking off seventh-ranked Auburn 24–10 in the 2006 Capitol One Bowl.

Which was the worst exit? Not Alvarez's—he was a victim of unfortunate circumstance. Not Crean's, since he wasn't the only coach to ever take what was perceived as an opportunity one couldn't refuse. Not Knight's, since it never happened. That leaves Favre, whose retirement ceremony was so emotional that his change of heart left Packers fans feeling empty. The ensuing drama that followed Favre and the Packers during the summer of 2008 and beyond made the purity of his original retirement announcement hollow, earning his exit the title of worst in Wisconsin sports.

WHAT'S THE BEST THING ABOUT WISCONSIN SPORTS FANS?

100 You hear it all the time—a coach or a player saying, "We have the best fans in the world." While some cities, some states, may have a good argument against the sports fans of Wisconsin, there are certainly no greater fans than the ones residing in America's Dairyland. Their passion for their teams is unequaled. The Brewers drew more than 3 million fans for the first time in 2008. Three million fans! The city of Milwaukee's population is about 600,000, and combined with the metro area, it's still fewer than 2 million people. To draw 3 million fans to watch baseball in one of the smallest media markets in the country is a testament to Wisconsin baseball fans. Anyone who watched the Bucks run to the Eastern Conference Finals in 2001 knows the Bradley Center can be a very tough place to play. The Kohl Center and Bradley Center give UW and Marquette a huge home-court advantage. The Badgers football team plays before a packed house of 80,000 fans at Camp

Randall on a weekly basis. Fans stay for a fifth quarter of dancing as the UW band plays on the field, win or lose. The Packers have a waiting list for season tickets measured in *decades.*

Wisconsin fans brave the elements. Anyone who's survived a Wisconsin winter knows it can be rough when the days are short. Yet the Packers fill Lambeau Field with more than 70,000 fans for every home game. Brewers fans tailgate no matter how cold, snowy, hot, or sunny it is outside Miller Park. The Badgers faithful are legendary for their ability to follow their team no matter where the venue is. Thousands of Badgers fans turned the Rose Bowl into "Camp Randall West" on New Year's Day in 1994. There were so many Badgers fans in Pasadena that year that organizers set up tents beside the stadium so fans who traveled to California without tickets could watch what was going on inside the Rose Bowl.

Sports fans in the state are fiercely loyal, and they are vocal. There's nothing like a Monday after a Packers game on sports radio in Wisconsin. In Milwaukee, three different radio stations carry postgame shows after Brewers games. In Madison, the sports talkers dissect every move made at UW. Sure, some of the Internet message boards can be a bit much, but the bottom line is that sports fans in the state live for their teams. The best thing about sports fans in the state of Wisconsin? Their passion.

SOURCES

The following books and resources were helpful during the research for this book:

True Blue: A Quarter Century with the Milwaukee Brewers by Chuck Carlson

The Milwaukee Braves, a Baseball Eulogy by Bob Buege

Packers Essential by Rob Reischel

Packers by the Numbers by John Maxymuk

Greatest Moments in Camp Randall History by Mike Lucas

The Baseball Encyclopedia

The media guides from the Milwaukee Brewers, Milwaukee Bucks, Green Bay Packers, Marquette University, and the University of Wisconsin

These websites were invaluable for statistical purposes: jsonline.com, Madison.com, si.com, baseball-reference.com, basketball-reference.com, and pro-football-reference.com

ABOUT THE AUTHOR

Carol Hunter

Andy Kendeigh is a sports anchor and reporter at WISN, the ABC affiliate in Milwaukee. He graduated from the University of Wisconsin, then worked in Madison before moving to WISN in 1999. He has covered the Green Bay Packers, the Milwaukee Brewers, the Milwaukee Bucks, the Wisconsin Badgers, Marquette, the Rose Bowl, the Final Four, the NBA Playoffs, the MLB Playoffs, the MLB All-Star Game, the NFL Playoffs, and NFL Hall of Fame inductions.